GOOD COP

GIRL

C○P 2.0

The Secret Life of Law Enforcement
What you still want to know about policing but are afraid to ask

LISA DOBLE

DEDICATION

This book is dedicated to my
loving husband Jason, and our three sons
Jack, Thomas and Joseph
who are always my biggest fans.

This book is also dedicated to
all law enforcement officers
that are on the frontline every day.

*** GRAB YOUR FREE GIFT HERE ***

The "C" Word: Confrontation
(5 Tips to Confront with Confidence)

FREE Download

https://www.lisadoble.com/free-stuff

** WARNING **

This book contains coarse language
and some real life examples of
police work that some people
may find offensive or disturbing.

It is *not* intended for shock value but
for educational and motivational purposes.

Reader discretion is advised.

TABLE OF CONTENTS

INTRODUCTION

Most people dislike cops. Think back to the last time you saw one . . . were you getting a ticket, driving by and watching someone else get a ticket or get arrested? Either way, most people are overcome with some sense of dread when they see a cop. Police are not exactly popular, and most people don't want to see or deal with them unless the shit hits the fan.

Let's face it, there are people out there that hate cops, and sometimes I must admit I can see why. There are police out there that are rude, power tripping assholes, and then there are others (like I was) that are firm but fair. I was nice all day long and treated people like human beings, regardless of what they had done (to a point), but bullshit me, or fuck with me in any way and it was game over.

This book aims to take a deeper look into the lives of law enforcement officers and how they think, how they operate and why. In this book I am going to show you that cops can be "normal," and they are really just trying to do their jobs. Most police I know are dedicated professionals with courage and integrity, and despite working in a thankless occupation, they still show up when called.

Of course, there are some dickheads out there, and police are no different. I bet if you thought about it you would either know, or know of a cop that should never have been given a badge. Thankfully the bad seeds generally get weeded out in some form or other. Hopefully!

After spending fifteen years on the front line, as a police officer in Australia, I would like to think I know a thing or two about police work. This book aims to build on my first book, *Good Cop Girl Cop: The Secret Life of a Police Officer*, by showing a lighter side of police work, and to show that cops are just like anyone else, but they have a crazy unpredictable job to do.

Police can be hated and disrespected by the general public, sometimes with reason, but mostly due to a lack of people's understanding. This book will also show you that it's not just the bad guys (and girls) that have all the fun. Police can make mistakes, use poor judgement, and get up to some ridiculous antics themselves, and when you add people, cars, guns, and animals, you never know what will happen. Yes, that's correct, I am going to expose a huge secret . . . cops are human!

I have seen some pretty wild stuff after fifteen years as a cop, and I am writing this book to not only entertain you, but to give you a greater understanding of police work and the people that do it. The stories and examples contained within are at times light and funny and at other times they are heartbreaking. But they may give you a new appreciation for the boys and girls in blue and help you understand what police go through.

Of course, there are many, many things that I cannot write about, if I want to stay intact. I have seen police commit crimes, I have seen corruption; and I would be a complete fucking liar if I said that I hadn't. Luckily, those assholes are a rarity, but they are there. Most police, with any lengthy amount of service, would have likely seen crime and corruption too. I am not going to stick my neck out and get my head cut off for anyone, so I will leave that right there.

If you liked my first book, I promise you will love this one too. This book has more of the same funny, sad, wild and bizarre stuff, but digs a little deeper into what a career as a cop really looks like. I promise, if nothing else, you will again be educated, motivated and entertained. Law enforcement is a gritty occupation that definitely rubs off on its officers, and basically, once a cop, always a cop. It brings a unique set of skills, and a very real element of danger with it. It can also leave a scar, literally and emotionally.

Police officers are put into extreme and highly unpredictable situations every day, and squeezed out of their comfort zones. Police have to gain control and take charge of situations, or what good would they be? Imagine police turning up to a car accident and freaking out at the sight of blood, or going to a brawl and being too afraid to break it up?

Most police continue to take their bold and brave attitude into their personal lives too; it is inevitable. I have been out of the force for a while now, but I still act like a cop. I see details, I notice things, I am suspicious and I can spot a dangerous person or situation. Those are not bad life skills to have.

But you don't have to be a cop to be kick-ass. So, how can *you* have that same take charge attitude and get shit done? You don't need to throw on a gun and uniform; you just need to be informed, be courageous, and stick up for yourself (at all times).

This book is easy to read and will have you drawing on the skills that police use to stay strong, in control and take charge. It also has some fun facts at the end of each chapter, and I guarantee you will be entertained, and hopefully learn something. The last chapter, "The C-Word Confrontation," has my top five tips that you can start to work through today.

Don't be the person who sits scared shitless and never gets out of their comfort zone. Don't be the person crippled by fear and afraid to speak up and take advantage of new opportunities. Be the person who grabs life by its giant balls and runs with them. Be the person who takes a chance, makes a change, kicks ass and takes names.

What you are about to read is raw, honest and completely true. If you have read my first book, you will know that I curse like there's no tomorrow, so this book contains R-rated bad language and factual (and at times disturbing) tales. If you find this offensive, then maybe this is *not* the book for you.

For everyone else, let's grab life by the balls.

CHAPTER ONE

Why Would You Want To?

I didn't have a lifelong dream to be a cop. I'm not like my husband who couldn't think of anything else he wanted to be since he was a little kid. I did well in school, but at the time I couldn't decide what I wanted to do, and as you may already know from my first *Good Cop Girl Cop* book, the cops ended up winning out.

People could not understand, and they asked, "But why would anyone want to be a cop?" Why would you put yourself through that, and join a profession that is either totally misunderstood or downright hated by people?

It took me a long time to actually find my calling, but once I decided to do it, nothing and nobody could stop me. I was laser beam focused on being a cop and for those that didn't like it or agree, too bad. I was going to do that anyway. I had no interest in opinions or advice from fucking idiots that had no idea about life outside our small town, and I couldn't wait to get to the academy.

What I never thought about until actually quite recently, was how my decision to do such a dangerous job would affect my family. I was so wrapped up in myself that it never crossed my mind that my parents might not be so excited about it. But that's the beauty of being young, you don't usually know, care or think about what is going on around you.

I know my parents trusted my judgement, but shit, when I think back, I was young, somewhat stupid, and selfish to pick such a dangerous occupation. But I can honestly say, I never thought about the danger. I never went into it thinking I would get hurt. Of course, I knew it could happen. I wasn't quite that stupid, but it wasn't at the forefront of my mind.

Like I said, if you have read my first book, you will know exactly what ride you are in for. If you haven't read the first one, no big deal, but it will fill in the blanks. This book builds on the first, and explores what it means to live a life of law enforcement, and gives you more of an insider's view on what cops go through daily at work and in their personal life.

But it's not all about the bad guys and girls. Police also do some stupid things and yes, I am included in that shit pile. Nothing done with malice, just sometimes without thinking things through. Police have to do something to pass the time and blow off steam when things get heated. Cops like to pull pranks on each other; well I do anyway, as it keeps it fun and interesting.

Of course, there are some cops that give everyone a bad name and let's face it, are just fucking corrupt. I am not going to go into that seedy side of cops behaving badly, as I like to think they are in the minority, and their bad behaviour will get flushed out eventually. But I can show you how cops are human and do stupid things like the rest of the population.

The Good Stuff

There is no other job like it. I have worked in quite a few places, a few different industries, and lots of different locations, including overseas, but there is no job like law enforcement. I have still never been as content with any job as I was with being a cop. Hands down, best job ever . . . for me.

Being a cop is fun, it's exciting, every day is different. Even if you went to the same type of job on the same day, they would be different. The people, the sounds, sights and smells are different. The outcome is also different.

Take a car accident as an example. You might get called to an accident where some dickhead had a bad case of road rage and decided to ram the poor unsuspecting victim, that didn't even realize there was an issue. Well . . . dickhead came off second best, after swerving at the car, missing it, over-correcting and hitting a pole. Hmmm . . . sorry no sympathy there from me.

Next accident same day, was a guy that drove head on into a Kenworth and ended up in the grill, like a piece of roadkill. Fucking hell! But this wasn't another case of road rage or a game of chicken, the guy actually drove into the truck to kill himself. Not much sympathy there either, except for his poor family.

So, wait a sec. Didn't I just mention that the job was fun and exciting? Well it is but unfortunately it can also be deadly, dirty and downright disgusting. But more of that later, back to the fun bits.

Comfort-Free Zone

The job is action-packed, and full of surprises and for me, it was the perfect occupation. See I get really bored doing the same thing day in day out. I can't cope. Once I know how to do something, I get really fucking bored with it (cast your mind back to my bank days in the first book!)

Police work cured that. I must be the type of person that likes a challenge and needs a certain amount of unpredictability to keep me interested. The work is certainly interesting, challenging and rewarding, sometimes all at once, sometimes not. It pushes you out of your comfort zone, forces you to speak up, take charge and control a situation.

You can't sit back, take shit or take a backward step. It's all you. People are looking at you to solve this shit situation, whatever it may be. This can be particularly scary when you are working one-out, with no back up, anywhere. It is all on you.

Imagine getting called to a domestic violence incident, where everyone is pissed to the eyeballs, or drugged out of their fucking brain, and you rock up by yourself and wrangle the perp to the ground, while everyone else is trying to take a piece of you. Now, can you see the challenging, action-packed, interesting argument? Is it rewarding at that moment . . . probably not so much, just happy to survive!

So, you can see how being a cop takes a certain type of crazy. Luckily, I had that and still do. My police attributes have followed long past getting out of the job. I was a cop for fifteen years, so it would be stupid to think that it didn't stay with me. And I like to fight, but don't tell anyone.

"So, what else is good about it?" I hear you ask? It seems like you are not convinced that policing is a great job. How about driving cool cars, high speed driver training, shooting awesome weapons, hand-to-hand combat training, and all the amazing gadgets on the duty belt. That was probably the bit that stung the most when I left, and had to hand in my stuff.

The Not-So Good Stuff

Whilst police work is not for everyone, it is a great career. But it is not all flashing lights, shootouts, and unbridled action. There are parts of the job that suck ass. My main gripe is shift work. Working 12-hour night shifts can really take the shine off an otherwise amazing occupation. Now night shift has its perks, but it's the cons that outweigh them.

I liked working nightshift for a few reasons such as, having no big bosses around, being less busy during the week (weekend nights are a whole different ballgame), and being able to catch a snooze here and there. Let's be honest, it's just not natural to be up all night, especially when you have to go home to three small kids at the end of shift. But on the whole, night shift is a grind.

The hours can be very long too. When you are busy and going from call to call, the time passes quickly, but once you make an arrest, you are off the road and in for a juicy amount of paperwork. It was torturous when we had to do this manually, typing up endless copies of fact sheets, charging sheets and bail applications. But once it went it to an online charging system, it was still fucking shit. So much digital paper-work!

So, what the fuck do cops do in between calls? The short answer is, patrol. You may get allocated an area to proactively patrol, maybe a crime hotspot, or a traffic accident blackspot. And in between, you drive, drive and drive some more. I have had shifts where I have literally gotten into the car at the start of a shift, and driven the entire time.

When I first started in the force, we worked eight-hour shifts, but in an effort to reduce the overtime caused by arrests at the end of a shift, they increased them to twelve hours. In theory, it's a great idea. In practice, you still got arrests at the end of the long shift that were supposed to be passed onto the day shift. Sounds great, until you realize the day shift had an arrest already too. And you had been driving all night.

What Day Off?

Then, there is missing out on family events, such as weddings, and birthday parties because you have to work. And yes, even if you ask for the day off in advance. It can be really hard to get a day off when you work in a team-based roster environment; you work the same shifts as your whole team.

If you are lucky enough to get the day off, or take a vacation, you have to also be prepared to be called back from leave to attend court or to assist with a major incident, like a natural disaster. That is very annoying when you have taken a few weeks off, and you get a call midstream that one of your court matters is listed and you are required to attend. This happened on a regular basis and can really fuck with your personal life.

Public expectation and media scrutiny are also at the top of the list of things I hate. All the fucking armchair experts that criticize the cops for anything they do. It is easy to be judged by the public, and then the media get a hold of it, and here comes a shit storm.

Of course, police at times make mistakes, but hindsight is a great thing when you have time to sit back and go through a scenario, casting judgement. Try making a split-second life-or-death decision when you are being shot at, and then come back to me with your opinion.

The public expect a fucking miracle; the media beat shit up all the time to make a good headline, and opinions are like assholes, everyone has one. But this is to be expected. You can't be a cop and be all precious about being criticized. Did it piss me off? Yeah. But did it make me do my job any differently? Nope. And I didn't give a fuck anyway.

It can be annoying when your face is plastered all over the front page of the newspaper, and they didn't get your good side. Or being chased down the street by TV reporters to get the inside scoop on a trial. I know the media have a job to do, but seriously, fuck that microphone off out of my face.

Another side effect of the job is cursing. I swear like a trucker. I didn't grow up that way, but when you work with criminals all day, and you are among people on the street, you pick up the talk of the street. I am not saying for a minute that you have to curse, but it does make you more relatable to the people you are dealing with, and it is a part of police work for most cops.

I remember being at my parents' place early on in my career. I was with my husband Jason (who was also a cop) and we were chatting about a court matter. The F bombs were flying thick and fast, and my dad was looking on in horror. He said to me, "Do you guys always talk like that?" and I answered a resounding "Yes." He accepted it and never mentioned it again.

They are some of the shittier parts of the job, not to mention the danger, risk of death and the reality of being injured. So why do people still sign up to do it and put their life on the line for others? I found my calling and policing suited my need for a stable, respectable career where

I could use my strength and courage to do some good. No idea what other people's motivations are, but mine was simple. I joined because I wanted to.

I hope that explains what may lead a person, like myself and many others, to want to join the force. Even though most people can't understand why the fuck you'd do it, I guess the job does attract a certain type of person that is looking for something.

Read on to find out about some of the bizarre shit that I came across in the city, and some of the equally fucked up shit that came my way when I started working in the country. And was city policing more dangerous and action packed than in the country? Well, you will just have to read on to see which is better. You might be shocked!

ARE YOU SERIOUS?

In 2019, the National Law Enforcement Officers Memorial Fund advised that over 21,000 law enforcement officers have died in the line of duty, since America's founding.

CHAPTER TWO

City Versus Country

People automatically assume that police work must be more dangerous and more exciting in the city than in a country location. I don't agree. They are both exciting, weird, full of action and drama, and I can't really say that one is better than the other. They are both equally challenging; it's just that you might face different things.

City locations have all types of people from far and wide, with at times transient populations, and a certain degree of anonymity. Country areas tend to have a more stabilized population that can go back generations, where everyone knows each other. This is absolutely a generalization, just to highlight my point. It is not always the case, at all. Expect the un-expected, in country, city or even out to sea!

During my fifteen years of being a police officer, I worked in a variety of country and metropolitan stations. I started off in the city (Sydney, Australia), where it was all action, almost all the time. It was a huge wake-up call being young and from a small town, and I soon found out how the other half lived.

Drugs, murder, assaults, suicides, and robbery were just part of the daily duties. Not to mention the peacekeeping duties of protests, riots, mardi-gras and large brawls. I loved the action of the city, and the fast pace, but after working there for a few years, I met my husband Jason (who was also a cop) and we moved to the country.

I wouldn't say that I prefer one over the other. Both city and country policing have their unique elements, and you have to be flexible and adjust to it. I liked being a cop in the city, and I liked policing in the country, but for different reasons. I worked at a bunch of city stations all around Sydney, and gained valuable experience at each one. I also worked at different rural stations of various sizes, each with their own quirks.

The city was a great place to learn the ways of policing and get some invaluable life experience. I loved the action, meeting all kinds of people from all walks of life, and with all kinds of problems. But the country kept calling me, as it is akin to the way I grew up, and I could get a horse again.

I had started riding horses at about age twelve, so the mounted police seemed like a natural progression for me. While I was still working in the city, I booked my riding test, but when I discovered I would have to commit to another four years working in the city, I changed my mind. I had just done three years and was eager to get out of there by then.

City Lights

The city was an exciting place for me to start life as a cop. It was a very steep learning curve, not just learning how to do my job, but learning about life in general. The city generally has higher crime rates than the country, largely due to the population density and the diversity of the residents and their ways of life.

So how does that contribute to crime? I'm glad you asked. When you get a bunch of people from different corners of the globe, living in close proximity with differing standards and beliefs, you can have a recipe for disaster. Throw in a tourist element, transient residents, and a level of anonymity, and you get the picture.

The city brings out some colorful characters that you generally don't see anywhere else. People from all walks of life might gravitate towards city areas where they are more able to blend into the environment, without anybody giving a fuck what they look like, what they do, or who they are.

One of the more memorable and colorful characters was the Phantom Shitter (that you might remember from the first book) who could crap in his hand on demand, and throw shit at the cops. Then there was the guy that walked around picking food out of bins, while covered in ferrets. Fucking ferrets! He said they were his only friends. Fuck me.

Another that comes to mind, was an old drunk guy that was arrested and brought in for causing a disturbance. My husband was working in the city charge room when this guy was brought in. When Jason asked him to empty his pockets on the charge room counter, he produced a white plastic shopping bag.

Jason asked him what was in the bag and he replied, like a fucking parrot, "fingers and toes, fingers and toes, but you will never find his head." He wasn't joking . . . the bag contained severed fingers and toes, and no, they never found the head just in case you were wondering. It turns out he was pissed off at his roommate and decided to kill him.

Allegedly, he threw the head off a bridge but thought it would be a good idea to keep the digits. I am not sure what he was planning to do with the severed bits, and I don't think he knew either. Jason was just glad that he stopped with the fingers and toes, and didn't cut the guy's dick off. Imagine booking that evidence. Ten fingers, ten toes, one cock. No, I cannot explain this, nor do I understand it; it is what it is.

City Crimefest

People may enjoy a certain level of anonymity in the city, and some people gravitate towards city areas to get lost in the sea of faces. If you lived in a country area and decided you wanted to dress up in a purple hairy fat suit, like Grimace, then you would likely stand out like dog balls in a country town, but in a large city, nobody usually bats an eyelid.

This can be an environment that is very conducive to committing crimes. The large and dense population combined with the larger amounts of banks and businesses than would be found in more remote areas can lend itself very well to the criminal element. More people, more businesses, larger economy can equal more opportunities for crime.

Of course, with the larger metropolitan areas, also comes the larger police presence. Police officers in city areas are generally better resourced than their country counterparts. Now I don't mean that city cops have guns and country cops don't. They usually have similar, if not the same personal equipment, but city cops have access to all the other specialty sections of the force and can access them quickly.

When working in the city, I regularly had the need for a dog squad vehicle to flush out a suspect, or mounted police for crowd control during a brawl. They were just a radio call away more often than not. Not that they *don't* have dog squads or mounted units in the country, but you had faster access to them in the city.

In Australia, our police forces are state based, and we have one federal police force. Therefore, the resources are spread across the whole state, so obviously most of the specialty units are based in the larger cities, like our State Protection Group (which is the equivalent to S.W.A.T), and the main mounted police and dog units.

The good thing about being a city cop is that you can have a certain level of anonymity. Most of the cops I knew commuted into the city for work, which meant they were not rubbing shoulders with the criminals they were arresting, and their personal and professional paths rarely crossed. Except for that one time when I found a stolen car in my unit complex.

I had just been down to the local pizza shop and the owner said he was having a shit day. I asked if there was anything I could do, and he said "Yeah, find my fucking MG convertible; some asshole stole it from the repair shop today." I told him that one appeared in my parking garage, and it was covered in a sheet. He came up, we looked under the sheet and fuck me, it was his car.

I called it in and while we waited for the local police to arrive, an unsuspecting tow truck driver came and loaded the car up. He was pulled over by police up the road, told that the car was stolen, and subsequently gave the police the unit number and phone number of the guy that ordered the tow. The bad guy got locked up, pizza man got his car back and I got free pizza from then on. Not a bad outcome!

Country Air

The city was good but Jason and I are country people at heart, so we decided to take a rural posting, the first of many. The country is great; the space, the pace and the air. But a rural posting can bring its own set of challenges and again, you have to adjust to a new demographic and a new way of working.

For starters, when you are a country cop, you are generally living among the people you serve. Let that sink in for a bit. You are living in the same town as the people you are arresting, charging and taking to court. This is definitely a major downside that can be daunting at first because, guess what, that means they usually know where you live.

Oh yeah, and your kids go to school with theirs; you shop at the same stores; you bank at the same banks and eat at the same restaurants. It's so awesome and opens a world of fun times, especially if you piss someone off just for doing your job. Yes, it can be a tricky balancing act to be local law enforcement and local resident simultaneously.

Jason and I found that out the hard way, when we moved to a two-man station, and he arrested half the football team, which he also played in. Awkward. There were a few smart asses that thought they could threaten him to see things their way, but if they weren't acting like fucking idiots to begin with, they wouldn't be in that situation.

It was very hard for us to have any privacy or anonymity, due to where we lived. We lived at the police station. Actually, our lounge room was the old court house, and the bedrooms were the old court offices. The police station was attached to the house, so it brought a new meaning to the phrase *working from home*.

I didn't mind it except for the fuckwits that would come and knock on the door at all hours of the night, usually drunk, asking for a ride home. My response was usually something like, "No" and when they would explain that the last cop used to give them a ride home, I would say something like, "Get off my fucking porch, before I kick you off it." If they were able to get their sorry asses to the local bar, then they could make their own way home.

When you live and work in a small town, you have to adjust to your new surroundings and fall into line with the way things are done there. Usually there are fewer services and less back-up than big city policing, and you have to basically become a jack of all trades. There are not usually the specialist units to fall back on, and when you are out on a call, you are it. All the decisions fall back on you and if you get in the shit, don't turn around because there's nobody there to help.

Working in a small rural community certainly gives you the inside scoop on everybody and their business. When attending calls, you are going to see friends, neighbors and other locals at their worst. The trouble is, not only do you know all their personal business, they fucking know yours. Or they think they do. Small towns, you gotta love 'em.

Small Town Sleuths

If you are not fourth generation born there, you are considered an outsider, and they are naturally suspicious of newcomers anyway, not to mention new police. It takes some time to get to know the community and gain their trust. Anyone that has ever lived in a small town will know that if people don't know the information, they will just make it up. Like the old saying . . . if you farted, by the time the message gets across town, you've shit yourself.

Country police have to wear a lot of hats, and sometimes there is no time to figure out which one. You might be going to a call as a cop; then driving the ambulance to the hospital while the paramedic works the patient; then assisting the medical examiner with an autopsy. Although the pace of work is usually slower in the country than in the city, you have to have a broader knowledge of all the things that big city cops have special units for.

One advantage though to having a bunch of town gossips, is that they can significantly help the crime clear-up rates. If you want to be a career criminal, a small town is probably not the best way to go about it. Like I said, everyone knows everyone else's business in a small town and nobody minds their own. If someone has the balls to commit a crime in a smaller town, the perps are usually flushed out by the community, one way or another.

One thing that does totally suck about living in the police station in a small town, is that you are never really off duty. In metropolitan areas, you can basically do your shift and go home. Not in a small community. The public expect you to be available 24/7 and 365 days, and it's hard to get away from work when work is your home.

You have to be equally interested in getting someone's cat out of a tree, and settling a domestic dispute. You have to give it the same attention, because if you don't, your ass will be grass with the townsfolk, and if they get a set on you, you are basically fucked, and nobody will tell you a damn thing.

Just because you wear a uniform doesn't mean that you will instantly get respect from people. I think a lot of cops fuck this part up, and think that they are owed something by being a cop. You're not owed anything; you are just wearing the clothes. You earn the fucking respect, just like any other person.

And just because you are sitting in a police car, again doesn't automatically mean that you will be respected. You are a road user, just like everyone else, and that being said, you are also open to all the perils and pitfalls of being a road user. You won't believe some of the mishaps and fuck-ups that happen to cops in their patrol cars, coming right up.

THAT'S CONFUSING?

American police forces are organized locally, Australian police forces are organized by state (except the federal police), whereas police forces in Europe, Asia, Africa, and South America are nationally organized. Clear as mud?

CHAPTER THREE

Car Trouble

Are police cars like normal civilian cars? Yes and no. Yes, because there is nothing special about the actual vehicle itself. It is not fitted with bulletproof windows; nor is it made of automatically bulletproof panels.

They are generally regular cars, that can be smashed, crashed, rolled and have tires shot out. Police vehicles can have ballistic panels fitted in the doors, but this is seen more often outside of Australia. Most cop cars have rolled off the production line in Detroit with the rest of them.

The only time the vehicles themselves (especially Aussie cop cars) are anything more heavy duty, is when they are purpose built or modified for a particular role, such as an armored vehicle used for bomb disposal or S.W.A.T. operations. Police vehicles can differ from normal civilian vehicles, but the modifications are probably not seen, unless you get in one.

Driver Training

Police vehicles are essentially used for patroling the streets, high speed pursuits and conveying suspects after arrest, taking them to jail, or escorting them to court. Police are trained to drive an array of police vehicles, such as sedans and SUVs, or sometimes more specialized vehicles. I have fond memories of my first stint of driver training when I was a recruit at the police academy.

I couldn't wait to get to driver training, as I love driving and I love cars, but the day it came around, I was nervous. I didn't know what to expect. I had heard all kinds of horror stories from the recruit classes that went just before we did. Some of them were just making up bullshit to stir people up, like if you make one mistake you get kicked out, and other stuff was actually true.

We had to drive an obstacle course, that made the one you did at the DMV for your licence look like a fucking pre-schoolers day out. We had to drive on an oil-filled skid pan, and actually lose control of the car on purpose. We also had to drive a high-speed pursuit, where we chased another vehicle around a track with lights and sirens going.

So what, you say? Seems easy enough right? And it was, but it was fucking nerve wracking when your name got called. I was extremely happy when I passed and then found out that you didn't get kicked out at all for failing; you just had to do it again apparently. But fuck me, some of those recruits should have been booted out.

If you can't drive or don't like to drive, it makes it horribly difficult to be a cop. Unless you are a beat patrol cop, a mounted unit or ride a bicycle, then you are likely going to be driving . . . a lot. Luckily, I love driving, which came in handy later when I was doing twelve-hour shifts.

Police Cars Versus Normal Cars

Like I said before, police cars start off life as a normal car, and the modifications you likely won't see, unless you become a "customer." Police cars are fitted with upgrades and accessories to suit a certain purpose; otherwise cops couldn't do their job. Imagine if a patrol car didn't have a cage divider between the cops and crooks?

You wouldn't want to be driving along with a bad guy right behind you, ready to choke you out with your own handcuffs, would you? Or to put a perp in the back seat only to have them climb over and sit on your lap? Hell, no and that's where the dividers come in handy.

Police cars also get fitted with all kinds of shit, like radios, lightbars, radar, license plate readers, fancy push bumpers, dashcams, sirens, torches, batons, shotguns and other weapon mounts, laptop computers, and very fucking cool stickers, just to name a few little extras. Police vehicles are modified to suit the needs and duties they are set to perform.

Pursuit vehicles might have high performance engines and modified braking systems. A K-9 unit would be modified with some sort of caged area to secure the precious cargo of the police dog (which students at the academy were told they were lower than, remember?) You can clearly see why a police car costs a shit load of money to outfit.

Not to mention the other shit they usually carry like a fire extinguisher, first aid kit, gloves, some basic riot gear and anti-bacterial gel to wash away all the nasties. Some police cars also come with a shovel, rope and a bag of lime to dispose of the real shitheads . . . joking, just seeing if you're still with me? Or am I?

The Trouble with Police Cars

So, what happens when that expensive piece of equipment, the police vehicle, gets in the shit? Or more to the point, when the driver gets the police vehicle in the shit? Yes, it happens, and often. Police are not immune to having car troubles, and when you are doing all manner of extraordinary duties and spending long hours in a car, it is not hard to see how this can fucking easily happen.

The following did not directly happen to me; however, I was there in the morning muster when we were all sternly warned to check our vehicles, inside and out before signing them out and taking them on the road. Seems like a fairly simple request from the duty sergeant, to check your vehicle for damage and contraband before you get in it. A previous shift had driven from our city headquarters across multiple precincts to collect a suspect for interview.

When they arrived at their destination, they opened the rear of the caged vehicle to place said suspect inside and convey him back, only to find a dead guy laying in the back of the truck. It seems that the shift before them had done a sweep of the streets, and collected all the drunk and disorderly homeless folk to take them to a shelter, but shit, they forgot one. And no, I don't know how that could have happened, but happen it did.

When I was still working in the city, I worked with a bunch of guys that loved horse racing. One particular guy, who was a very experienced officer, inherited a rookie. About the first lesson to the rookie, was to go and put some bets on. This was before the days of phone betting apps. He was listening to the races on the car radio, while the rookie was driving.

They came to a stop at a major intersection, and the race loving guy was so into the race he began to yell, "go, go, go." So, the rookie who thought he was talking to him, went straight into the intersection, crashing into other cars. The moral of the story: It seems that driving while listening to horse races is a health hazard.

Now my husband Jason, was a cop too. And we worked together at the same location, and on the same vehicle, a lot. People cannot believe that we would work together, nor could they believe that the police department would not only put us at the same station, but on the same car crew. Most people freak the fuck out and say they couldn't handle it, but we didn't know any different. We worked together on the first day we met.

Don't Try This at Home

I was however, very glad I was not working with him on the few times he had "car trouble." One day (during our time at the piss-ant small, two-man station) Jason went out into the state forest with a cop buddy that had brought a rifle over with him to have a test shot. The rifle had two triggers.

Jason was asking his buddy how the double trigger system worked as he had not seen a gun like that before. The guy attempted to explain it, but got the instructions mixed up. As a result, Jason accidentally shot a round from the rifle, which went straight through the front guard of the police car.

He almost got away with it, by placing a piece of white tape across the bullet hole. He had a friend in a nearby town that had a car body repair shop, where he was going to have it fixed. Before he could get it repaired, another officer borrowed the car and noticed the piece of tape, which he removed. Poor Jason . . . there was no way he could get out of that one.

Another time, when I am *glad* we were not on shift together, he was patroling in that same rural area, and went to drive into a paddock with a local farmer to put away some sheep that had got through a fence. As they drove into the property, he unwittingly encountered a very deep and muddy trench, where electrical workers had been out the day before laying cables.

The car went in and down to the police stickers on the side. Jason jumped out of the driver's window and ended up waist deep in mud, up to this gun belt. The farmer jumped out of the passenger window and came around to help him. He grabbed his arms, and yanked him out of the mud, right out of his boots. Jason's boots are still buried down deep in that trench.

Now I can't be picking on Jason the whole time, as I have had my share of car troubles. I was working with the duty officer, who was the rank of inspector, out the back of nowhere, ten miles from somewhere and near the corner of fuck knows where, pulling out drug crops. Marijuana plants, over six feet tall, and a lot of them. We were tired, sweaty, dirty and smelt like Bob Marley's ashtray.

The car had plants sticking out of it and was covered in mud. It was an SUV, so it was perfect for four wheeling and pulling up plants. The duty officer was driving, and we were heading back to our station, when he saw a large mud puddle on the side of the road. He thought he would be a hero; actually, he was just being a smart ass and decided to swerve into the puddle to "wash" the vehicle for the next guy on shift.

It turns out that the "puddle" was actually a ravine full of water, and down we went. I was amazed at how quickly a car will fill with water. You see it in the movies, but the water literally started gushing into the car the minute we went in. I thought the car would keep going down and that I was going to drown.

I remember pulling my feet up and getting right up on the back of my seat, as we were going down, while the muddy water had reached the police radio. I quickly told the duty officer, to get the windows down before the electronics were fucked. The car by now was almost vertical and I told him if it moved another inch, I would be jumping out the window.

To my surprise, the vehicle came to a stop, with the rear bumper still high in the air. Luckily, one patrol unit was driving past and saw the ass of the car sticking up out of the water. Someone swam in and put a tow rope around the back of it and pulled us out.

The car was full of water up over my lap, and just like in the movies also, I opened the door and it gushed out. The only thing missing was a couple of fish. The car was a write off, as all the electricals and the engine were damaged, and did I mention the vehicle was also brand new? I am so glad I was not the driver that day. We got exactly one week's use out of it before it was fucked.

Ride Like the Wind

I do, however, have a story where I *was* the driver. I was the senior officer, working with another female officer, on patrol about 3 am. I saw a guy ride a bicycle down a side laneway, behind a row of shops, in the main street of town, so I stopped and waited for him to ride back out. He was up to no good, fucking snooping around at that hour, scoping out shit to steal.

As he rode out from one of the lanes, we swooped on him. He saw us and was riding like a bat out of hell to get away. He was riding his bike on the sidewalk, as we drove along the street urging him to stop. It was all good. I knew who he was anyway. A regular (thieving) customer. I really wanted to stop him as I knew he would have a bunch of stolen crap on him, but he wouldn't slow down.

I came to an intersection, and I thought I would accelerate and get around the corner in front of him, so we could jump out and get him off the bike. I did accelerate. I did get around the corner and hit the brakes to get out, and I did stop him. I just didn't stop him the way I had planned.

He was going so fast, as I turned, he swerved to get around the vehicle, and hit the back of the police truck. I remember looking out the window to see the guy and his bike cartwheeling across the intersection. And right as I said to my workmate, "Fuck I hope I haven't killed the prick," he jumped up to his feet, grabbed his bike and took off riding.

I said, "Fuck it, if he is that keen to get away, he can keep going." About an hour later, another officer came up to me laughing after stopping the bike riding bandit, riding fast and furiously on the way out of town. He asked him why he was riding so erratically and the guy said, "Two of your crazy bitches just tried to kill me."

Sorry, but I thought it was funny. I will just add it to my shit list, and hope I am not going to hell for it. At least when you fuck up in your own vehicle, mostly, nobody knows about it, but when you fuck up in a cop car, everyone knows about it.

It's the same with animals. If something stupid happens to a cop that involves something with fur, or feathers, everyone's going to know about it. You can't get away with shit being a cop. Sometimes the animal kingdom works against you, and makes you the butt of jokes for a good long while.

But sometimes animals can work for you. In this case, I am talking police animals. Check out this next bit to see the times I have been in a scary predicament, and other times when animals have been my bestie and helped me get the job done. Unfortunately, probably mostly scary shit though!

WHAT THE FUCK?

The Japanese police experimented with a device called a Motorcycle Arresting Device to stop members of biker gangs, whereby the bike literally ran over a device that basically grabbed the wheels and stopped the bike. Go figure!

CHAPTER FOUR

Paws, Claws, Feathers And Fur

You know the old saying, never work with kids and animals? There is a reason for that. They either let you down, make an idiot out of you or can be just plain dangerous (the animals more so than the kids). I have encountered all types of claws, paws, feathers and fur both in an unexpected capacity and as part of the job, with police dogs and horses.

As a cop I have encountered just about all kinds of animals, from chickens to goats, sheep to kangaroos, cats, horses, pigs, cattle and don't forget dogs. Dogs can be a major hazard to a cop; even police dogs can be an issue if you don't know the rules around them and their handlers. Like rule number one, don't touch the fucking dog! Some dumb cops do.

Ask any cop if they have ever been chased, bitten or simply confronted by a dog, and I would be shocked if any of them said *no*. Dogs are the main type of beast that I have come across on the job, that have caused the most problems and been the major cause for concern. Now, I am in Australia, so the number of man-eating animals is limited, compared to living in the U.S. where I would be more concerned with running into a fucking bear.

Sure, we have some of the deadliest snakes and spiders on the planet, and my American friends are always amazed at how we get to adulthood here, but the only thing that would really come out and eat ya whole, would be a croc. And thank goodness, the only crocs around me are in zoos. So back to man's best friend, also known as canis lupus familiaris, or the domestic dog.

Canine Capers

There are times when the humble dog has stopped me or my fellow workers from doing our job. I can think of two occasions that really stand out where I was luckily not injured, but scared to death, panicked, shitting myself and went to water. I love dogs, but as a cop I fucking hated dogs. You're a stranger walking into someone's yard, into the unknown, when all of a sudden out comes a dog. Make that two dogs. They were fucking rottweilers.

I shit myself. I walked into a front yard that had a high brick fence all the way around, to keep people out and the dogs in. I opened the gate, started walking to the front door, and there they were. Big, black, beastly and fucking angry. They were both staring me down, growling, drooling, and creeping forward.

My partner went to fucking water and hid behind me. I was not much better; the adrenalin was pumping and we had nowhere to go. I had hoped that the dogs' owner might have heard the commotion and come outside, but shit, he wasn't home. All I could think to do was to keep eye contact, (which I am told is about the worst thing to do because dogs fucking hate it) and back away slowly.

That's all we could do. We slowly backed up to the gate, until we could get through it. It felt like an eternity, but eventually we got out of the yard and were standing in the driveway, counting our fingers, toes and blessings. Then the owner arrived home and I explained that his fucking dogs nearly shredded us and he said, "Oh, they won't hurt ya."

About a week later I was out working with Jason when we arrived at a house to serve the guy with a summons to court. We both got out of the car, and began to walk to the front door of the home, when out of the corner of my eye, I see a boxer dog head down and ass up, bolting straight at us. Again, I shit myself; this time I hid behind Jason, and he drew his baton ready to crack it on the head.

Just as it came leaping at us, with its fur all fuzzed up and teeth out, the guy came outside and called it off. We were lucky not to be torn to shreds right there, but the irony is, that the summons was for the offense of having a dangerous dog. Some fucking idiots just never learn.

Animal Kingdom

Apart from being bitten by little fluffy things (the *big* dogs are scary but I have only ever been bitten by the *little* fuckers), I have also walked into a house and had a bat fly into me, found a pet wombat in someone's bed during a search warrant, and my husband Jason has been chased by an emu.

Not to mention rogue pigs, sheep, horses or cattle running through carparks, and shopping centers, or a house full of snakes who had been let out of their cages. Feathers, fur, wings, claws and paws can be a health hazard to a cop, but it is all part of the job and you have to be prepared for whatever comes at you.

Of course, there are animals that help police do their jobs, such as the mounted police and K-9 units. I do regret at times that I didn't join the mounted police. I should have done it, as I had been riding horses my whole life, but I wanted to move out to the country even more. At least going back to a country station allowed me to have my own horse again.

Police Horses and K-9 Units

Mounted units are great to have on hand in protests, riots and brawls. They have a great vantage point and can spot the trouble makers easily, being they are up so high. They have the added advantage of being able to pin people against a wall, or against another horse, until backup arrives to make the arrest.

And, a lot of people are shit scared of horses in general, so they can be quite daunting to the uninitiated. Police horses and riders are highly skilled and trained members of the force, and they can go places and do things that a vehicle or person on foot cannot do. If only I had my time over, I should have turned up to that riding test and at least tried.

Another valuable member of the police force is the police dog. I love being out on calls when a dog arrives to assist. Again, dogs can do what we mere mortal humans cannot. I mean, imagine if I bit some asshole that I was trying to arrest. You don't fuck with police dogs.

They are highly trained and the handlers are highly skilled in controlling the dogs. You don't call out to them, don't try to direct them to do anything, and don't ever fucking touch them. The dog and its handler are a complete unit, and nothing should get in between them. Except the criminals, of course.

Police dogs are incredible to watch when they are working. When the handler gives them a command, they are on duty. Now this might sound cruel, but there is nothing better than to see a guy that you have been chasing in a foot pursuit, get taken down by a dog. They can't escape them. And most people are afraid of police dogs, and if they are not, they should be. Those things can rip you apart.

The bond between the dog and its handler is so strong that if a police dog retires, or if an officer leaves the dog squad, the dog usually stays with them. The dog is so in tune with that person, that it makes sense not to split them up. Police dogs are usually kept at the officer's home, and they are a huge part of the family.

My Own "Police Dog"

I was never in the dog squad, but I did take a dog on patrol at times. My own dog. Jason and I had a Rhodesian Ridgeback named Shumbah, and when we worked in that small town with the two-man station, he was the only dog available to help. People don't believe that we would take him on jobs for backup.

If one of us got called out at night to a prowler, or a brawl, Shumbah would be in the back of the police truck ready to help out. Nobody said anything. Everyone in the town knew who he was anyway. See, our dog had a bit of a reputation around town, and nobody was game enough to wrangle with him. He wasn't savage at all, but he would stick up for his family if needed.

When I kept getting called out to a prowler lurking around the back laneways, looking into people's windows, I thought I would take my dog. After all, the dog was huge, and you never know who or what you are going to run into. And when I couldn't find the bastard, he did. Before I started taking him on callouts, he would follow me and get there first anyway.

When you work in a small rural town, and you don't have access to a dog squad unit, you improvise. Shumbah was too big to mess with. Ridgebacks were originally bred to hunt lions. Generally, they would jump up and grab a lion by the ear and pull it to the ground. I saw Shumbah do this to a buddy of ours who came over for a visit.

Jason and his friend were mucking around, sparring each other in the back yard. The dog kept a close eye on Jason's friend and when he stepped in and tried to grab Jason in a failed wrestling move, Shumbah pounced on him. He grabbed the guy by the ear, dragged him to the ground, and drew blood. I was shocked, but he was protecting his family, and that's why we took him out on calls.

Shumbah was a character, and everybody knew him. He would sometimes disappear for a few days at a time, and we would find out he would go and "visit" people in the town and they would feed him. Then when he'd had enough, he would come home, or we'd get a call to come and get the "big red dog."

We also regularly got called up to the local school, after he would go there and play with kids at lunchtime. He normally did this when we went out for the day, as he didn't like being home by himself. He was very gentle with school kids, and the teachers didn't mind except when he would run off with the kid's soccer ball and not give it back.

My Dog the Thief

Shumbah was also well known in the main street of town, where he would often go and visit the shop owners, but I didn't know it at the time. One day he came home with a loaf of bread in his mouth. I naturally thought he must have snagged it from somebody's trash bin, until I went down to the local market and they filled me in.

He had walked down to the shops with the kids and I before, but I would tie him up outside. Apparently, he came down on his own, walked into the shop, grabbed a loaf of bread from the shelves and ran out the back door. I was not sure I believed the shop owner at first. I thought he was taking the piss out of me that my dog was stealing fucking bread, come on.

Until one day, I got home and there was a large plastic bottle of milk on my doorstep. I thought the neighbor had dropped it off, as she was always trying to get me to buy milk off her milkman. Then I saw it had teeth marks in it. And when I spoke to her next time, she told me she had ripped the milkman a new asshole for forgetting to deliver her milk. I didn't have the heart to tell her it was Shumbah.

Shumbah was not only a character around town; he was super helpful on those callouts at night, especially when we worked by ourselves. One evening Jason got called to the local RV campground where the owner's son had been threatening her and her partner with a knife. He had just thrown his mom's new guy through a plate glass window.

Jason got to the campground, and the guy had his parents holed up in the office area with a meat cleaver. The guy had a long history of mental health issues and had threatened to kill them before. Jason called him out and he appeared with the meat cleaver, two large dogs and a spear.

He was threatening to kill Jason, and started coming towards him waving the meat cleaver. Jason pulled out his gun and told the guy if he didn't stop, he would shoot him dead right there. The guy kept yelling and waving his weapons around, and only put them down when Jason told him he would shoot his dogs.

The guy thought more about his dogs than about himself obviously and dropped his shit. Of course, Jason would have shot him before he shot the dogs. He was wrestled to the ground and spent the next six months locked up. But six months later, he was out causing shit again, and hiding in a cabin at the RV park at 2 am.

Jason responded, and when he got out of the car, he heard a loud thumping noise coming toward him. It was Shumbah running across the wooden bridge to the campground. Jason ran into the cabin and wrestled the guy to the ground. Shumbah burst in the door to back him up and grabbed the guy's arm. Ah, man's best friend.

It's not only animals that do silly things and make the job harder. Sometimes it's you or your cop buddies that act stupid and mess up, and hope against hope that nobody finds out, as you will never hear the end of it.

Mostly, it's all in fun and no harm done, but occasionally things go wrong. Stay tuned to find out some of the stupid things cops say and do. I would like to say I have never done anything wrong, but I am included in that. And you won't believe how cops in Thailand get punished for fucking up, coming up next chapter!

K-9 CHIHUAHUAS?

Chihuahuas have been used as certified K-9 units to detect drugs, execute search warrants, do school locker and vehicle searches or check inmate property at county prisons. Guinness World Records state the smallest police dog is Midge, a chihuahua cross and official Law Enforcement K9 in Ohio, USA.

CHAPTER FIVE

Cops Posing As Humans

Police are usually seen as these mysterious, faceless creatures that lurk about streets and alley ways looking for criminals. There is an air of mystery to being a cop, and most people just see the uniform, the gun, and the badge, and not the person behind it. Which poses the question, can cops be human?

Of course, they fucking can. They are, you just don't see it. Like all humans, cops can also make mistakes. I know it's hard to believe. I am being sarcastic here just in case you didn't pick that up, but it's true. Even the most well trained, smart and astute cop can get it wrong and fuck it up. And I am in that shit bucket.

Saying Stupid Things

Remember the old saying, never assume, because you make an ass out of you and me? The same applies for police officers. They are not immune to the odd slip in judgment, the odd distraction or sometimes just a bad fucking call. You start out with best intentions and aim to remain impartial, and look at situations individually and blah, blah, blah.

But when you have been doing the job for a while, and see the same kind of things and the same type of people over and over and over, you could be forgiven for thinking (at times) that all crooks are created equally. Why would this assault and battery callout be any different from the thousands before it?

But they are all very unique situations, with different individuals each posing various types of threats. It can be easy to get a little complacent, but you really can't afford to. One bad decision could literally mean your life, or the life of some poor unsuspecting person, so it pays to stay on point.

There are times when cops slip up, maybe due to complacency or fatigue but there are times when the bad eggs purposely make bad decisions. I have seen police officers act corruptly, I have seen some assholes commit crimes, but most police are dedicated, hard-working and full of integrity. I don't want to give air time to those scum that wear the badge, because those few bad seeds paint a shitty picture for the rest of us.

The law catches up to those bad seeds just the same as the general public when they commit a crime, and if anything, the hammer swings down harder. And so, it should. You take an oath to uphold the rule of law, to protect and serve the community. There is nothing worse than seeing a cop abuse the powers they have been given and take advantage of innocent people.

When a cop goes to jail, it can end quite badly for them, as you can well imagine. Here they are high and mighty, putting other people away, and then end up there themselves. Luckily, the criminals also have a code, and a cop in jail is like a fucking ant under a magnifying glass in the hot sun.

But I aim to show a lighter side of cops doing stupid things. Just to show that they too are human beings that get tired, sometimes can lack great decision making and do and say dumb things. I am not immune to this myself.

I once had to deliver a death message for a live person. What the fuck? Yes, you read that right, and in my defense, it wasn't really my fault, but I sure felt like a dickhead. I went to a call where the guy had hung himself in the garage. When we got there the paramedics were just in the process of cutting him down.

The paramedic informed me that he had been hanging there for a while, and they suspected he had snapped the brain stem. In other words, he was fucked. Unfortunately, he was a relative of someone I knew very well, and the boss thought it was best that we were sent around straight away to give them the bad news.

I delivered the news to the family. They were obviously distraught, and began to get themselves together to go and see the body, when I got a call that he was still alive. His vital signs had been so weak that they had been unable to detect a pulse or heartbeat while we were still at the scene. They eventually found one, but forgot to tell me straight away, before I delivered the news to the family. Didn't I feel like a dickhead?

Oh No You Didn't

I admit, like many others, I have opened my big mouth and spoken inappropriately (I know, you are shocked right?). I remember taking a phone call from some lady that was abusing the crap out of me for no reason and rambling on about shit to the point where I didn't know what the fuck she was talking about.

There were some other cops sitting nearby that heard me get a spraying from her for no apparent reason, and they were pissing themselves laughing. I needed a break from her bullshit, and pressed the phone down onto my leg and said, "This stupid bitch is fucking rambling on with shit. I can't understand a fucking word out of her."

After we all had a bit of a laugh, I put the phone back to my ear, and *she* said, "I heard you, I'm not a stupid bitch, thank you." I proceeded to tell her that I wasn't talking about her, I was talking about someone else, and she apologized to me! Don't judge me; it's hard being viewed as a glorified problem solver.

I'm not the only one that has said something stupid. I was working the front counter one night doing station duties when the phone rang. I was busy taking another phone call, so another officer walking by took the call. All I could hear was him yelling at the person on the other end, accusing him of being drunk, and told him to "sober up first" and then come in if he had a problem.

About fifteen minutes later an elderly gentleman came into the police station. He told me that he had just tried to phone up to report an incident, but the officer accused him of being drunk. It took all I had for me not to laugh, as I walked out the back to get the officer.

Now to be clear, I was *not* laughing at the old man, but instead the situation the cop was in when he realized that the "alcoholic old drunk" that he couldn't understand on the phone, was actually a poor old man with throat cancer. I don't care what anyone says, I think his fuck up was worse than mine. Wasn't it?

It wouldn't be right or fair of me to put my stupidity in the book and let Jason get off without a mention. Actually, I think him shooting the police truck a few chapters back would beat me hands down. But here goes. There was an old lady that lived up the laneway behind the two-man station we worked at.

Walk It Out

She was super nice, lived alone, was in her very late 80s, but still very spritely. She walked every day, and still drove a car. One morning while she was completing her daily ritual of walking down the dirt lane to go to the shops, she tripped and fell.

The poor old bugger laid there for some time, trying to yell for help. The back yard of the police station backed onto the laneway, and when Jason finally thought he heard someone yelling for help, he went out to assist. She was in a lot of pain, and complaining that she had hurt her hip.

Being a lifelong football player and no stranger to injury, Jason gave her the only advice he knew and told her to "walk it out." He got her get up and into her house. She became distressed as the pain was getting worse, so he called the paramedics. She spent the next good while in hospital with a fucking broken hip. Walk it out he said, shit!

Sometimes police just blurt out the wrong thing due to being tired, working long hours and putting up with draining people, but sometimes the things they say that are meant as a joke, can actually have the opposite outcome. Jason had made an arrest and had to take the suspect to the hospital after they had sustained a minor injury.

The suspect's friend also attended the hospital; however, the friend was not involved in the crime at all. Jason's colleague told her that she was going to go to jail right along with him. This was utter bullshit, as she wasn't involved at all. She was so distraught at the prospect, she jumped out the second-floor window of the hospital and ran off.

Doing Stupid Things

Do as I say, not as I do? I can't really give that advice, when you have just seen a snippet of the silly things police say (including me). But not only do sometimes inappropriate things get said, but also done. What can I possibly mean by this, that police can make mistakes? Hell, yes, they do.

When I was working in the city, my workmate and I got called to an assault at a bar at 7 am. I was wondering who the fuck would be drinking at a bar and brawling at 7 am, I mean we weren't in Las Vegas. We walked in and it looked like something out of a horror film.

There were unconscious patrons lying on the ground, covered in blood. There was so much blood everywhere; it looked like a murder scene, but it wasn't. There had been a huge all-in brawl sometime earlier and it appeared everybody was "sleeping it off."

As we were looking around the scene, totally shocked at the amount of blood sprayed everywhere, one guy woke up and jumped to his feet. He was obviously still drunk as he was swaying around, covered in blood. As we went to help him, he took a swing at us and simultaneously, my buddy and I both leg swept him.

Neither of us realized the other was going to do that, so the poor bastard got smashed into the ground and knocked out. His head hit the ground so hard it sounded like someone had dropped a watermelon. He didn't move and we thought we had fucking killed him. Luckily, he moved eventually.

I have also fucked up when I have been working alone. One night when I was shift supervisor, I was driving around late at night in a larger country town. I came across an elderly lady walking down the sidewalk, with an elderly gentleman on her arm. She was trying to hold him up and he was staggering all over the place.

I stopped to give them a lift home, and she told me he must have had a few too many beers at the local bar. I insisted on giving them a lift home, until she pointed out that they were literally right in front of their house. She commented that she didn't think he'd had very much to drink, and didn't need any help, and began to walk across their front lawn.

I left and started back on my patrol, when I got a bad feeling and drove back to check on them. He was on the ground, losing consciousness and the paramedics arrived soon after. The poor old guy was having a stroke and ended up dying. I had to go get his son, in the middle of the night and tell him that he died. There was nothing more I could do I guess, but I did feel really bad, as he was staggering due to the stroke not the beer.

Dead Weight

One time I was working with Jason (surprise, surprise) when we got a call for a deceased person. I don't normally feel anything much when I go to jobs, because you can't. If you had a feeling about every call you went to, you would be a blubbering idiot. You have to keep an emotional distance to do your job and survive.

But this job was a little sad. It was a pair of oldies that had grown up together and been together their entire lives. She had got out of bed early in the morning to make a cup of tea, as she did every day. While she waited for the water to boil, she started to sweep the kitchen floor and literally dropped dead. She still had the broom in her hands when we got there.

The old guy was distraught as you can imagine. We called some family to come and support him while the paramedics told him she was dead. A doctor confirmed that she had a heart condition and wrote a certificate, so the funeral directors came to collect her.

They zipped her up in a body bag and asked Jason to help carry her out. After Jason had tripped over her feet when we came in, he fucking had the head end and dropped her on the way out. In his defense, there is a reason they call it dead weight.

There are many other snippets I could tell, but we could literally be here all day. Like the time the old sergeant in the police lockup let all the prisoners out of the cells to make toast, because he thought they looked hungry. Then there was the time Jason angrily dragged a guy out a car, who was slumped behind the wheel. Jason thought he was drunk. He was having a diabetic episode, but I have one more story that I *have* to tell.

The Other Guys

Remember the movie "The Other Guys" with Will Ferrell as an anal police accountant and

Mark Wahlberg as his very frustrated offsider? If you are familiar with the film, you would know of the famous "desk pop" scene where Will Ferrell's character is encouraged by the cops to shoot his gun in the office, and pops a cap into the ceiling.

What I am talking about is not quite the same scenario, but let's just say it's the same result. There were two guys we worked with at one of the larger rural stations. One day they had to take a bunch of prisoners next door to the court house. While waiting in the back office to escort perps back and forth, they were bored and decided to play a game.

You can see where I am going with this. They were fucking around seeing who could draw the fastest, and spinning their service pistols around their finger like in a western movie. All in fun until someone loses control of their trigger finger.

Suddenly, one of them accidentally pulled the trigger and shot the wall in the court house office. They were lucky that the court house was very old, and the walls were very thick concrete which muffled the sound to a degree. People did still hear the noise and came running in to see what had happened.

The two of them sat there all sheepishly, and denied that anything had happened, saying they were all good. They were both fucking lucky that nobody got shot, and there was only two of them in the room, so they were able to cover each other's asses. If that's not a shit yourself moment, I don't know what is.

You could be forgiven for thinking that these guys were bored, and decided to have some fun by playing John Wayne in the courthouse. But fuck me, there are much better and safer ways to achieve the same result. Break the boredom that is, not shooting the wall.

Police work is not all lights and sirens; there's a lot of down time and waiting around, and cops get just as mischievous and take things too far at times, just like everyone else. Just because they wear a uniform, does not make them immune to creating a situation to shake things up.

If you are looking for some new and inventive ways to prank your friends and family, then check these out. Of course, you likely won't have access to some of the props used in the next bit, but maybe you do. That can just be our little secret!

WELL, HELLO KITTY!

The Huffington Post reported that mis-behaving police officers in Thailand are forced to wear an armband that is pink, with the Hello Kitty logo. Apparently, the police colonel got sick of warning way-ward officers, that didn't listen anyway, and the armband is meant to make them feel a sense of guilt and shame for their transgressions. Meow! That is all.

CHAPTER SIX

(Im)practical Jokers

You know the saying that necessity is the mother of invention? Well, so is boredom. If there is fuck all to do, but you have no choice but to sit and wait and do your job, then you better believe that cops will create something to do, or say.

But what type of jokes would a cop make, being that they are usually seen as serious and not having a sense of humor. Cops usually like dark humor to keep things light, and what better way to test out your humor, and to break your boredom than on your work colleagues.

Ever wondered what police officers do to curb frustrations and let off steam? Well they might feel like punching the odd suspect in the face, but alas, they cannot. So, what do you do? You are sick of all these assholes committing crimes, had enough of working late nights and overtime and you just want to have a bit of fun like a normal person.

Here is what you do . . . practical jokes. The hands-down best way I can think of, to decompress. I love a good practical joke. I love being the object of them, but better still I love playing pranks on others. Come on, I only do it because they want me to.

But what type of practical jokes would fine upstanding officers play on each other? You'd be surprised that most jokes that I have experienced are fairly benign. People expect that cops would do insanely ridiculous things; maybe once upon a simpler time we would but now with fucking body cams, dash cams and who knows where else cams, you have to be careful of what you say and do.

I like a simple joke where nobody gets hurt, and everyone including the butt of the joke has a laugh about it. I would not want to pull a prank on someone to belittle or bully them; it's not me to do that. I don't need to shred someone down to make myself look good; some might but I don't.

Police have a very full-on, demanding job. It can take a toll physically, mentally and emotionally, and when you are facing death, destruction and violence every day, you need to step back and have some fun to keep sane. Pranks help to build camaraderie and keep things light and fluffy when things get hectic.

Not So Practical but Very Funny

Take the good old, never fail, kick-me-hard sign. I have had many work buddies that were shit-stirrers but one guy stands out. He was always pulling pranks, talking shit and being a smart-ass. My kind of person actually. He decided to go up the street to the local café to get a coffee. As he walked by me, I was able to strategically and lightly place a kick-me-hard sign on his back.

He strutted up the street to get his coffee, thinking he was king shit, and wondered why people were staring at him and laughing. He was a plain clothes officer so it wasn't the uniform. As people snickered at him, he wondered what was so funny, and finally at the café somebody alerted him to the sign.

When he came back in the station with his coffee, he was screaming my name and calling me a "fucking bitch" while laughing. When I came out to the front counter, he had stuck the sign on his forehead and said, "Now I know why all those assholes were laughing at me."

Another favorite that most cops could relate to is putting pepper spray on the rim of the coffee cups. The amazing thing about pepper spray is that it activates with moisture. When you get sprayed (cast your mind back to my accidental spraying in the first book, thanks to you-know-who) it burns like a motherfucker.

You wash your face to eliminate the chemical and get some relief, but it takes ages to calm down. Even later on you can be feeling okay, and jump in the shower and bam, it fucking burns again, over and over. When you gently wipe it on the rim of a coffee cup, it dries and is basically undetectable.

That is until you make a cup of coffee and the moisture reactivates the spray and, you got it, it burns. Another cool place to put a shot of spray is in the car aircon vents. Small things amuse small minds, I guess.

Speaking of the cars, you never let an opportunity go by to pull a prank. Many a time have I got into a car and everything is subtly turned to the on position, just waiting for the ignition to be turned on. I'm talking radios at full volume, lights, sirens, and wipers and anything that has an on-switch or makes noise.

Once after working a very late night, I got back to the station with the sergeant, who was complaining all night about how tired he was. We were working a stupid Friday night shift that knocked off at 4 am so he was whining about needing sleep. I was driving and told him to go and unlock the station, and I would bring in all the crap that we had to carry.

He was grateful, and made his way up to the side door and as he went to unlock it, I drove up beside him where we normally parked the police vehicle, and hit the lights and sirens. He fucking woke up quicker than a junkie getting a shot of Narcan, and looked like a deer in the headlights.

He saw the funny side after his heart rate came back down and never complained about being tired again. I should just explain, Narcan is a drug administered by paramedics to counteract a drug overdose. A person can go from looking almost dead, to jumping around like a jack-rabbit within seconds.

Apart from other bits of silliness, like putting flour on top of the ceiling fans, moving the police car to another location (for best results use on rookies), or sending shameless emails from a computer left logged in, pranks just help to ease tensions and pass the time. It's all fun until someone like Jason, takes it too fucking far.

I hate mice. Not the ones that sit beside your keyboard, although they can be a useless piece of equipment right there. No, I am talking about live, mice with fur and claws. I hate them. Maybe it's from childhood when I would go to feed my horses in the dark, and the rats would run along the rafters over my head, or jump out of chaff bags.

Anyway . . . Jason caught a mouse while out on foot patrol one night. He put it in a McDonald's cookie box. When he came back in the station, he came over to me with a look that I knew all too well. I knew he was up to something, so I removed myself.

He went over to another female officer who was typing and asked if she wanted some cookies. I can't believe she trusted him and said *yes*, and he tipped the live mouse out on the keyboard. She screamed, the mouse fucked off, and I was so glad he didn't drop it on me. Filth.

I guess that was a fairly harmless prank, unless he did it to me; then someone would have been harmed for sure.

(Angry) Man or Mouse

It's funny how I would rather face an angry person than a mouse. At least he didn't put it in my locker. It's not unusual to find many random items in your locker like shaving cream, shredded paper or porno mags. That's if your locker hasn't been moved, turned upside down, or used to lock someone in and throw them down the stairs. Just kidding, or am I?

Let's not forget people farting in a small enclosed space and locking you in it, sticky tape on the inside of the phone mouthpiece so callers can't hear you, or the old fingerprint ink on the hatband. Yes, I know, fingerprints are digital now.

It was great when we used registered number tags instead of name tags. The tags were used to identify officers before name plates came in.

If you got in the shit, you would swap your tags around, so they were unable to identify the officer involved. Or if you were lucky to have one with numbers like 1, 0, 6 or 9, you would turn it upside down.

Practical jokes are great but they can keep you on edge, especially when you have pulled a prank on someone, and are waiting for them to retaliate. You don't know where, when or how. But some pranks are a little more subtle, where you have to set the bait, and sit back and wait.

There was this guy that was, to put it as nicely as possible, a complete and utter pain in the ass. He was nice enough, and liked a good laugh but could be annoying as fuck. The downside was that he also had a brother, so there were two of them to deal with. He was the perfect victim for my next prank.

Sign Me Up

I found an obscure old porno mag that had been lying around the station, after being taken off some dirty old perve that got caught pulling his dick in public. I used a pen to open the back page, as there was no fucking way ever, I was going to touch those pages with my hands. And there it was . . .

An advertisement graced the inner back page for the Enema Fancier's Society. What the fuck? Is that even a thing? Yes, it is. There are people out there that fancy enemas. Okay . . . but to have a club for it? That's next level.

I took down the details, and penned a beautiful and heartfelt letter from that officer, stating how he was so glad he found the society, as he has been keeping this secret for years, that he enjoyed enemas, and was too ashamed to tell anybody. Just to be clear, I am not criticizing anybody that likes enemas. I mean, go your hardest, whatever blows your hair back.

But keep that shit (no pun intended) private, for fuck's sake! Do you really need to have a club for it? I mean what the fuck do you talk about? I don't want to know. Anyway, I wrote the letter, filled out his information and posted it away. Then I forgot about it.

About one month later I was fortunate enough to be on shift with him, when the parcel arrived at the police station address. He opened it in front of everyone thinking that someone had sent him a gift. And he was all smiles, until he read the letter back from them, inviting him to their next meeting. Ah, some of my best work.

Other cool pranks I can think of that I have seen, is someone putting straight pins upside down into the office chairs. This is really fucking cruel actually when I think about it. You know a common pin that has a pin head on it, well you push the head of it down into the chairs, and the spiky end is sticking up.

Or waiting until someone goes into the bathroom, and throwing lit crackers into the toilet block. Again, that's pretty cruel and they mostly think they are under gunfire or a bomb has gone off. If you didn't shit yourself before, that will do it. Crackers in a confined space is never a good idea, and again probably best used on rookies. No haters please!

Taking It Too Far

Another prank that was a little more serious, and I personally would have run through a concrete wall if it happened to me, was the old rookie hazing at the morgue. My training officer took me to the morgue when I first started, and while it was interesting to a degree, (apart from seeing a guy cut in half) it still gave me the creeps. At least my training officer was a little sensitive about it and didn't pull any nasty shit on me.

Imagine the poor rookie that was taken there, into a room, with a dead guy lying under a sheet, toe tag hanging off him and stiff as a board. Imagine now that the rookie is encouraged to go in for a closer look, as the cop and morgue attendant tell him to pull the sheet back. As he goes in to have a look, the fucking dead guy (or cop posing as one) jumps up and scares the living shit out of him.

I would not have coped with that; someone would've got hit for sure. Someone almost did get hit the time I fake arrested my brother-in-law Ben. He had come to town with some mates to go camping, and they had never met us. It was New Year's Eve, and I set up with him to come down for a noise complaint.

I went over to him and told him to turn down the noise. Ben basically told me to fuck off, as it was New Year's Eve and started arguing with me (all a set-up). His friends were shocked that he was being difficult and arguing with me, telling him to shut up and do what he's told. I then went on to warn him he would get locked up if he kept going, and he did, so I arrested him.

I slapped the cuffs on him, and it was me, him and the old sergeant that knew about it. His friends were fucking horrified and tripping balls to say the least. We kept it going for a while, but it all become too fucking funny, and we all started laughing. The look on their faces was priceless.

Pranks are part of police life to keep things moving along and lighten up some dark situations. But that started before I even got to the station; at the police academy. Many a time somebody would come back to their room and find someone had either broken in, or got the key from security and messed shit up.

People would find their mattress in the communal bathroom down the hall, or all their shit removed from their room, or other people's stuff was jammed in there. Then there was the guy that got all his socks flushed down the toilet for being a fuckwit. Yep, that was my handywork. I may have had a few drinks on board.

And you thought cops would be all stiff and mature-like . . . hahaha. I know it's hard to believe but police do have a dark sense of humor and will resort to a practical joke to shake things up. But sometimes the practical jokes are not enough to keep things light.

Sometimes, the work goes home with you, and you'd be surprised the ways in which it does. Sometimes it is in the physical sense, like being followed by a bad guy, and sometimes your space gets invaded in other ways.

Read on to find out what shit cops sometimes have to put up with, after they have done their shift and gone home. It doesn't end just because you have taken your gun and badge off, and finished for the day. You are never off duty, and there's no overtime for that. Check it out!

OH NO, YOU DIDN'T?

Only around one third of a police officer's time is spent actually enforcing criminal law; most of the work of a police officer involves peacekeeping, order maintenance, and problem solving; hence the boredom and practical jokes. Proves my point!

CHAPTER SEVEN

When Work Follows You Home

Police work is gritty and hard, and can be long hours, so you definitely look forward to going home at the end of the shift, if you're lucky and don't have to stay back. But just because the clock is telling you it's time to go home, doesn't mean you are really off duty.

A cop is *never* off duty. Let that sink in for a bit. If you work in a traditional role, you likely do your job and go home and don't give it a second thought until the next day. Cops are different. You are always a cop, and you are always expected to act like a cop, whether on duty, off duty or on holidays. You are a sworn officer representing your police force.

The work can follow you home and creep into your personal life in more ways than one. I am not just talking about being physically followed home, which has happened to most cops at some time or another, especially if you live and work in the same town, or a town nearby. It can really happen anywhere; if the crooks are determined to find you, they will do exactly that.

Trust me when I say that just because you are a cop does not mean that people don't have the balls to front you at home, or follow you in your car. Of course, when they are doing this, they are obviously thinking in the now and not paying a thought to the possible consequences. You can have your fifteen minutes of fame now asshole, and make threats to me when I am off duty, but that won't just end there.

Honey, I'm Home!

Work can follow you home in a physical sense, where you are actually followed by a creeper, or it can invade your social media or personal phone, in the form of messages. You can be accosted by assholes when you are on a day off minding your own business, or you can bring home bad memories from a bad callout.

Oh, yes, there are a myriad of ways that police work and personal life intertwine, and I have encountered most of those ways, or I know someone close that has. Sometimes it's just plain annoying; other times it's something that puts you in a predicament, or at worst it can be deadly.

When you are a police officer, you are effectively placing a target on yourself and there are people out there that would like to see that target hit right in the bullseye. When cops get threats against them, it is easy to laugh it off and not take it seriously because it happens so frequently. They always "know where you live, what car you drive, and know where your kids go to school."

Seriously, if you panicked every time somebody told you they would kill you, or will "see how tough you are without your gun" you would be a nervous wreck. But every now and then, they do follow through with their threats and you have to pay attention. You just have to be smart, keep your eyes open, expect the worst and hope for the best.

I recall a time when I was pregnant with one of my three boys. I was station bound as it is unsafe for a pregnant woman to be frontline, out on the streets. I always laugh when I watch the movie Fargo, with Frances McDormand as Margie, who is a very heavily pregnant police chief in a snowy Minnesota town.

I am not sure about other police forces, but certainly in mine, as soon as you were pregnant you were taken off the street for safety reasons. I can't imagine seeing a real-life police woman working the street, with a huge baby belly, dressed in uniform. I am not saying that doesn't happen; it just didn't happen where I came from, and I certainly wouldn't do it.

Anyway, I was pregnant and working the counter in a nearby larger station, when I decided to go up the street to the pharmacy.

Jason was off that day and just happened to be driving by the pharmacy as I was being abused by two teenage boys. They recognized me even though I was not obviously in uniform, and began calling me names like pig, slut and copper dog.

The pharmacy was literally only one hundred yards from the station, and Jason stopped his car, got out and led them by the ear back to the station. He called the kids' father in who was pissed off at his sons being taken to the station, until he found out what they had done. Let's just say it didn't end well for them and leave it there.

Win Some, Lose Some

Being a cop can cause you to lose some friends, and gain new ones. There are certain people in your life that just don't want to stick around once you become a cop, because you might interrupt their criminal activity. It can be hard when someone you know well is up to dodgy shit, because you cannot put yourself in compromising situations.

Before you become a cop, you might go to a party and people are toking on bongs, or worse, and you just ignore it, but when you are a cop and meant to uphold the rule of law, to serve and protect, you can't fucking put yourself in those predicaments. You don't want to be standing there, as a law enforcement officer, when the place gets done for selling drugs.

There are certain people that cops cannot associate with, and that would be known criminals for one. You have to be very careful of what you do in your personal life that could impact your career. Oh, and you will likely forever be introduced as a cop, even after you leave, so you better get used to it.

When I was a cop, the first thing that came out of people's mouths was "Lisa is a cop." Even now, since leaving the force, when I meet new people or go into a new work environment, they still lead with, "Lisa used to be a cop." I know the job is a little different to a normal day job, and I guess it's my own fault for continuing to write fucking books about it. I mean there are worse introductions, right?

I mean you wouldn't introduce a new person and say, "Hey, Mary used to be a cashier." I get it, the job is kind of out there, but to a cop, it's just normal. It would be very hard for most people to understand what police actually do, and how they can normalize it, but it is what it is. Someone on the outside looking in might just see a cluster fuck of gigantic proportions, but again, to cops, it is just their job.

I have had the unfortunate experience of knowing police that have been involved in a tragedy, while on duty, that has crossed into their personal life. I worked with a young guy in the city, who moved out to a country station not too far from me. One night he got called to a fatal car accident, and when he arrived at the scene, he saw his wife dead in the driver's seat.

A fatal car accident is a very, very unpleasant experience to say the least. I think the thing that gets me the most is that it can literally happen anytime, to anybody. You don't need to be a scumbag or a criminal. You don't need to necessarily be doing the wrong thing either, to lose your life in an instant.

One minute you are driving along, sipping on a coffee, (or not, like some Aussie states that have made it an offence to do so now) and you are laughing, joking and chatting to a friend about what you are going to do on the weekend. One mile up the road, you are wrapped around a tree, and not going anywhere, ever again. Just like that.

Sometimes you don't know the people that have died in an accident, but the work day can still invade your personal life. When I was working in the city, a call came in for an industrial accident at the local subway station. Thank fuck I did not get this job.

Dead Meat

It's not a nice thing to say, but it is easier to justify the death of a person if they were a shitbag, drug dealer or pedophile (especially a pedophile). I don't normally judge people for their choices, and criminals are people too, that can get dragged into shit. It's easier to accept though that a serial rapist got popped, rather than a cute little old lady.

But police sometimes justify the death of certain people in an effort to protect themselves. Except a pedophile. I do not speak for all cops here, but I personally will never, ever be sorry for seeing a pedo get killed and I don't give a fuck what anyone thinks. If you had seen the things I have, you would be of that opinion too.

It is awful to think you were just going about your day, until you're not. It's a brutal way to go, and I have seen my fair share of dead bodies in cars, but for this guy to get a call to a fatal, not knowing anything about it, and finding his wife, that's adds another level.

It seems a guy was just doing his job and loading trash into an industrial shredding machine. A large piece of trash went into the machine and it got stuck. The worker climbed into the machine to remove the obstruction, which subsequently caused the blades to start up again.

He became human mince-meat. That is one fucking gross callout. Those poor guys that attended that job, came back looking green, and I remember sometime later, one of them telling me he had never eaten meat since.

Again, this takes me back to Fargo, where the guy put his buddy through a woodchipper. You get the picture! The amazing and ironic part of that juicy story, was that they found a four-leaf clover in the man's wallet. Poor bastard, no luck was had on that fateful day.

One call that I did get was a police-involved shooting at a nearby jurisdiction. If you've read my first book, you'll remember the mad woman with two knives, who was shot dead in her own driveway. As if that's not enough to deal with, that job followed the officer home, too.

The officer involved in that shooting woke up to some shitbag spray painting their wooden fence at home with the word "murderer" in red paint. Then, as if that is not bad enough, the fucking media splashed it across the front page of the newspaper.

That's just some of the shit you have to deal with as a cop. When I was a kid, my dad was a bricklayer, and he had a buddy that he worked with all the time. As kids we went to their place for barbecues, and friendly visits and they came to ours.

Imagine my surprise when I went to their house to assist with executing a search warrant for drugs. I didn't know the address until we got there, but I didn't think they would recognise me, as I hadn't seen them since I was a kid. Remember that wombat in the bed . . . that was this place.

Doesn't Play Well with Others

Being a cop can also cramp your social life if you are in a smaller town. There are only so many bars and restaurants to go out to, and invariably if and when you do, you will run into your clientele. Some police are actually restricted from attending certain bars in their own precinct.

We were not actually restricted from it, but who would want to frequent the places every other idiot goes to. The last thing you need is to be enjoying a quiet drink, or a nice meal with your family and get approached by someone you have arrested. Now, can you see why cops usually stick together?

Social withdrawal is fairly common among police. Due to the nature of the work, you can't mix with certain people; you don't want to frequent the same places as the people you throw in jail and people generally don't understand what you do. After all that, you just get sick and tired of people and their problems in general, so it is easy to become a hermit.

Not long after I left the police force, I started a new job in employment services. One of my first clients came in and said, "You don't remember me, do you?" After an awkward pause and trying to remember who he was without any success, he stated, "You arrested my son." I got ready; I thought *here we fucking go*, and then he said, "It's okay, he deserved it."

There are other ways that police work can clash with your personal life. When I was a cop, we were not allowed to work in the security industry on licenced premises, such as bars and hotels. We also had to get permission to work a second job.

The reason being was that your new job might bring the department into disrepute. Imagine an officer having a second job as a stripper? It's not a good look. You arrest someone during the day, and at night they are slipping dollar bills into your G-string.

It may not seem that fair, but it is. It would be very easy to exploit and take advantage of your position if you were then working in those areas. For example, if police were working security in a bar, it would be viewed as a conflict of interest. The department would be worried about bribes and corruption, if they were to keep the licensing police away from the place.

It can suck at times being a cop, with all the rules and restrictions, and dickheads throwing death threats around. Or while you are in-directly mingling with the criminal element (kids playing in the same footy team). Even when minding your own business, you just can't get away from the job.

Now, I love going to the cinema, but I will still say, police work gives you a front row seat to the greatest show on earth. Sometimes I would arrive at a crime scene and want to grab a bucket of popcorn and watch the show. Human beings can put on the best show and entertain without even trying.

You are never off duty, so when shit goes down in front of you, you respond. Whether you are working or not. This expectation, responsibility and lack of fucking down time can get a bit much at times. Combined with the daily tragedy and public scrutiny, it can all come crashing down.

It's a shame that cops only get paid for their actual shift, because like I said, you are never off duty. Combine that with assholes trying to follow you home, bring you down, make a complaint and just be fuckwits in general. It can be hard to get up each day and keep going with it.

There are times when it does all become too much, and you don't fucking feel like getting up for it at all. The job does take its toll, regardless of how tough you are. Whether it is stress, fatigue or intolerance, everyone will be tested in some way and sometimes to the extreme, as you will see, coming up!

WHAT'S IN IT FOR ME?

In the USA in 2019, 66 % of police departments reported seeing declining numbers of applications, according to a survey of four hundred law enforcement agencies by the Police Executive Research Forum (PERF). I'm shocked! (Insert sarcasm here.)

CHAPTER EIGHT

When The Job Takes Its Toll

Mostly cops are quite good at self-care and making sure that things don't pile up on them too much. A lot of cops use heavy exercise (like me), some use alcohol or other shit to escape and others escape life altogether, which is an all too common occurrence.

You can't be a cop for any length of time, and not get affected in some way. On the lower level, cops are intolerant of people, unsociable or withdrawn. Then there's the ones that are shitty at the world, and bring down the vibe of everyone. Of course, at the extreme is police suicide which is literally the end of the road.

With all the duties, action, responsibilities and perils of being a cop, it is easy to see how the work follows you home, but what about when it follows you home and takes up residency? I mean this in the metaphorical sense, not meaning a scumbag actually coming and living in your house, which I am sure has happened somewhere in some form or other.

No, I am talking about the ways that the job can catch up to you, grind you down to the mat and hold you there if you are not careful. Any cop that has worked in this job for any lengthy amount of time can attest, that it takes a toll on you in some form or other. Whether it is a physical, mental or emotional sense, I am sure most cops feel that the job has taken a little part of them.

Personally, I feel that night shift aged me. I mean I don't quite look like a weather-beaten old sea hag, but I do think it aged me. When you are deprived of your beauty sleep and forced to sleep during the day which is so fucking unnatural, I don't care what anyone says, it just aint right.

Stress

I am sure there are people out there that love being a night owl, but I am not one of them. But the number one issue cops face (apart from being shot, that is), that can really take a toll or can take your life is stress. Stress is a killer. We all know that. But add that stress to a volatile, highly demanding occupation with the constant threat of death or injury and you can see why it's fucking hard to be a cop.

So, where does the stress mostly come from? Well, you would be surprised to know that *many* cops, (I'm not so stupid as to say *all* cops) but many cops will tell you that the bulk of their stress comes from departmental bullshit, not necessarily the stuff from the streets. Yes, you read that right. Many cops will tell you, including me, that there is a lot of pressure applied from within your own department.

Why is that, you ask? Well, the short answer is that policing is largely driven by politics and public opinion. Policing can be shaped politically by rising crime rates, statistics and knee-jerk reactions from the brass. Throw in the media, and public scrutiny and you can begin to understand the pressures that can be applied and felt by cops.

I am not for a minute saying that stress does not come from the callouts that are attended. Of course, there is stress involved there, when you attend a critical incident, and have a gun shoved in your face, or someone wielding a machete. It is stressful to attend a domestic disturbance with one or both parties being completely off their chops, and waving weapons around.

Anytime you make an arrest, it can be stressful and physically draining, if you are in a foot pursuit, wrestling a person to ground or having a stand-up fist fight. It's fucking draining, and you have to be on your game and ready for anything at all times. Draining, draining and draining.

That is exactly why physical fitness is paramount in this job; well it was to me at least. If I was going to be doing all that shit, I wanted to do it at my best. Stress is an absolute prick of a thing that can lead to fatigue, anxiety, depression, addictions and insomnia. These afflictions can strike anybody, but police can be more prone to them, based on the demands of the job.

But telling a person not to stress out is like telling someone with anxiety not to worry, or someone with depression not to be sad. It can creep up and bite you in the ass before you realize the fucker is there. Have I ever felt stress in the job? Of course, I fucking have, and again, exercise was my go-to.

Post-Traumatic Stress Disorder

Being exposed daily to danger, real threats on your life, trauma, death and the misery of humankind, can and does have an impact. Sometimes the impact is even greater and can lead to post-traumatic stress disorder (PTSD) and in the worst-case scenario, police suicide. The problem is that cops are great at giving advice, and telling people what to do and solving their worldly problems. Cops are fucking shit at doing that for themselves.

It is *your* job to solve people's problems, and make split second decisions. It can then make it hard to take advice when you are the one that gives it. Most cops fear seeking help for PTSD, as they can feel like they will be seen as being weak, or just trying to pull a police pension. PTSD is rampant, not just in policing, but also in other emergency services, due to the graphic frontline work.

It can be triggered from one traumatic incident, or it can be an accumulation of many traumatic incidents over time, that can build up and lead to suicide in some cases. Unfortunately, I have known of many officers that have either taken their life, or tried to.

Police Suicide

I remember one day when I was working in the city. It was a normal day, working with our normal day shift team, when there was a "call" to the male locker room. My husband Jason was working on the same team as me, so he was there that day. He went into the locker room with some other male officers, to find a colleague with his service revolver in his mouth.

Luckily, they were able to wrestle him to the ground and disarm him without anyone getting hurt. It's fucking bad enough dealing with shit like that out on the street with random people, but when it is one of your own, it puts the wind right up you. It was sad to think, had they walked in there a few moments later, it may have been a totally different outcome.

Others have succeeded in killing themselves with their own gun. And there have been some that have hung themselves or cut their wrists, after being severely traumatized by the job. This job is the real deal, it's not some Hollywood movie bullshit; it's real life and it can chew you up and spit you out.

There are other less dramatic ways that policing can take a toll on a cop and those around them. We have all seen the Hollywood portrayals of the divorced, alcoholic cop on the edge like Mel Gibson's character Riggs, in Lethal Weapon. I would like to say that marriage breakdown and alcohol dependency is all bullshit when it comes to cops, but I can't.

They are just some of the real issues that can affect police families as a result of the physical and emotional demands of the job. And no, this does not happen to all cop marriages and families, but it does happen. I had a double dose of cop life in my family, being that I was also married to a cop, but we survived because we had both walked in each other's shoes. Just lucky, I guess.

Police Subculture

The police subculture is alive and well. It can be hard for cops to relate to other people that are not police, because you work in a unique and hostile environment that most people would never know of. Just being a police officer can scare some people off and make you socially isolated and unsociable.

I was first given the idea of becoming a cop by two guys I had worked with in the bank. They had joined the force, and I remember asking one of them if it affected their social life. His response was, "No, it improves it." It didn't, that was bullshit, for me anyway. I think he meant you just do more socializing with cops.

Some of the reasons why cops can become unsociable are because the callouts can make you suspicious, desensitized, prejudiced, cynical and mistrusting, with no faith in humanity, hypervigilant, burnt out, and never off duty. Oh yeah, cops can be so fucking fun at a party, right? When you are carrying all these burdens, you just can't be fucked with people. Sad, but true.

You also know things that you really wish you never knew. You know all the dirty little secrets of your kids' school friends, like the mother who works at the local clothing store and got charged for embezzling profits, or the father who stabbed his best mate to death during an argument.

I am not sure if it's a good thing or a bad thing, but you also know who all the sex offenders are. I mean that is a good thing to know (my kid won't be going to that fucking kid's birthday party) but it also makes you jaded. And the kicker is, you can't fucking tell anybody about it, because even those pedophile assholes have a right to privacy. Fuck me.

I can recall, (I better be careful here) a prominent person who had molested a disabled teenager in another town, and it was all caught on CCTV. Sucked in you fucking piece of shit. This really pissed me off, as he was married and getting around the town like his shit didn't stink, and yet there was this dirty little secret. Disgusting piece of shit.

It gave me an immense amount of pleasure to return his property to him that had been confiscated on the night in question, when he was arrested and charged. It was a toiletries bag, that I could have just handed over to him, but I made him come in the station, and tipped the contents out on the counter, as the property receipt was itemized (insert smirk here).

The dirty fuck had a little molester's kit that contained condoms, lubricant and other small sex toys. Now any other poor unsuspecting idiot would have gained front page news status, but not this bastard. Fucking Teflon, no mention of it in the papers anywhere, and it did not affect his job at the city council because nobody fucking knew about it. So frustrating to keep quiet.

Knowing Too Much

I know the job made me hypervigilant and over-protective with my boys. They never had sleepovers when they were young, and I was always careful of where they were going and who they were going with. I always encouraged their friends to come to our house, so I could keep an eye on things.

And once I left the job, I struggled as many cops do, with a loss of identity. I joined the force as a fresh-faced twenty-year-old, and when I left at thirty-five, I was lost. I was not a cop anymore, and I felt like I was standing at the edge of a very large cliff with nowhere to go. I had been a cop basically my whole adult working life, and when that was gone, it took me a long time to accept it and figure out where to go from there.

I wish I never knew some of the fucked-up shit that people do, because it can be quite disturbing to know what is out there living among us. I would ordinarily say that whatever people do behind closed doors is their business, but the problem is that I have been behind those closed doors. The job took me into people's homes and into their deranged lives and trust me, it's not always a great place to be.

I wish I didn't know as much as I know about death, like the fact that you lose control of all bodily functions, and generally piss and shit yourself. There goes your dignity. But worse still, is knowing what the inside of a body looks like. Being present at an autopsy is quite disgusting, and no I don't find it scientific or fucking interesting. Quite the opposite, and I would rather be anywhere else.

I wish I didn't know about the weird and not wonderful sexual things that people do for money or pleasure. Some things are laughable and just plain weird, and other stuff is un-imaginable, like parents pimping out their kids to pedos or uploading kiddy porn of their own children for money. Just when you think you have seen it all, you haven't.

There will always be trailblazers and those idiots seem to somehow find other like-minded individuals. How these sick fucks find each other is just beyond me. Like a mother that decides to let a guy blow his load over her child, as long as he doesn't penetrate her. Seriously, how the fuck do you bring that subject up to someone? Bloody hell! I don't want to know.

I know I have just made policing seem like the most grotesque and beastly occupation known to man. I have pointed out a lot of negatives and the ways in which the job can beat you down. But at the end of the day, I don't regret my choice. I still loved every bit of being a cop, and I enjoyed it until it was time to go.

It gave me some very unique experiences and I learned so much along the way. My eyes and mind were open to things that I never would have known. Some amazing things and some fucking terrible, nonetheless they were my experiences. I would still recommend the job to anyone that wanted to give it a go.

I would not even dissuade my boys if they were keen to become police. It is a job like no other and allows you to watch the greatest show on earth, and get paid for it. My best advice though would be, when you have had enough of it, you leave. It took me fifteen years to get to that point, so it must have been okay!

If you have endured all of that bullshit, over the course of time, then you have likely seen a lot of changes in the force. Sometimes it's the constant changes that can be a source of stress also. And sometimes it seems there is change just for the sake of it.

I've seen my fair share of changes in the force, over the fifteen years I was there. Some of them good, some of them stellar, and some maybe should have just gone in the shit bucket right from the start. If change is for the greater good, and is actually helpful and adding value, then I am all for it. But if it's just for shits and giggles, count me out. I am certain that sometimes people in authority change things up just to keep themselves in a job. Read on to see some of the changes I have experienced, and you be the judge!

YOU'RE JOKING, RIGHT?

Police officers are at a higher risk for suicide than the general population. More police officers die by their own hand than are killed in the line of duty, due to a range of contributing factors such as officer burnout and depression, and their reluctance to utilize counseling and referral services.

CHAPTER NINE

Now And Then

Police work is police work. Right! It's the same shit every day, making arrests, charging suspects and going out to do it all over again. So how can it possibly change? Well, it does and often. The core principles of the job are the same and that will never change, but the way things are done, certainly can.

The policies, procedures, legislation, the equipment and even the types of criminals and crimes they commit do change over time. When criminals are finding new and inventive ways to commit their crimes, then the police have to keep up in order to be able to catch them. Bad guys can be very resourceful, and cops can be the ones playing catch up.

If you want to be a cop, you better get used to change. If there is ever a job that is a revolving door of different opinions, stats and trends that change the course of your work, this is it. There are the old dinosaurs of the job that will resist it with all their being, but at the end of the day, change is inevitable, especially in policing. It can sometimes seem like someone is always moving the goal posts on you.

Focus areas fluctuate with crime trends, and those trends can fluctuate based on who has recently come out of prison or been sent to prison. Other factors—like which season of the year it is, and current opportunities for crooks in the crime hotspots—force the police to have to move and adapt to keep up.

Policing has come a long way over recent times, and I have seen many changes myself from when I joined the force. Way back in the day before there were police, people basically policed themselves and dished out their own forms of community justice. As policing evolved, the early cops were volunteers who did it out of a sense of civic duty and to protect their families.

The purpose of police is to maintain law and order, and prevent crime while remaining impartial and only using physical force as a last resort. These are just some of the Peelian principles, adopted by Sir Robert Peel that outline some of the standards of an ethical police force, particularly in the United Kingdom, Australia, New Zealand and Canada.

Change, Change and More Change

They say that necessity is the mother of invention, but it can also be said that necessity is the mother of change. When things don't work the way they should anymore, you find a solution. I can think of one of the major changes in my police force coming about out of necessity, and the need for change after a tragic incident.

For more years than I care to remember, officers in my police department were issued a Smith & Wesson .38 six shot revolver. I thought I was king shit of turd island the first time I fired a weapon. It was an amazing blend of what the fuck, oh shit and damn that was cool, but with the utmost respect at what it was capable of.

Many of us referred to them as a pea-shooter, because accuracy was not always on your side. They had a range, where they were accurate enough, but let's just say they are better for closer range work. Anyway, they were cool, but a fucking pain in the ass to reload, especially when you were under pressure, like getting shots fired at you.

Do You Feel Lucky, Punk?

Just like in the Dirty Harry movie where Clint Eastwood's character Harry Callahan asks the punk if he shot 6 shots or 5, and asked him "Do you feel lucky punk, well do ya?" Same thing for cops with revolvers. You better have an idea of where you are up to, especially if it's dark, noisy and raining.

You have to have your wits about you. I can't imagine pulling the trigger when you are counting on that bullet to come out of the chamber, and it shoots blanks. We had these little black rubber strips called "speed strips" (not the best name for them really) that house six more rounds.

You had to carefully peel them into the chamber, without fumbling and dropping them, and yes, I have done that, just in case you wondered. Imagine my relief when we finally got a usable, functional, 15 shot Glock semi-automatic pistol, Model 22. Perfection (that is actually the Glock slogan, not mine.)

Now, instead of having a maximum of 12 rounds available with a revolver, we had 30, counting the 15-round magazine, and the spare mag. It took a little bit of getting used to, and the loss of some hand skin when the rack slid back to chamber a round instead of revolving, but it's a lesson quickly learned.

I was grateful, as were most cops for the increase in firepower, and accuracy with the new Glocks but they came at an awful price. They came about due to two fellow officers being shot and killed. They attended a "routine" domestic disturbance, (which are categorically anything but routine) and were confronted with some asshole wielding a large caliber rifle.

Out of respect for the officers involved and their families, I won't go into too much detail, but they were basically cornered, ran out of rounds and were outgunned. This was in a fairly small country town where things like this never happened. Until they did. At least some good did come out of their tragic deaths, and the police force responded, but it is a tragedy that this had to happen at all.

Other changes in equipment were born out of a desire to make things more functional and practical for officers. When you are carrying a shitload of extra pounds of equipment on your duty belt, every little bit counts. Duty belts are not exactly the most comfortable item of attire I have ever worn.

Little and Large

We used to have these ridiculously long and bulky spun aluminum batons, that looked like a giant stick of salami. They were such a pain in the ass, and very fucking dangerous really as they were not overly secure on our gun belts. They were held in place by a large metal ring, with a rubber stopper that gave it some form of security, but they were easily grabbed by morons.

Cops are taught to place a hand over our weapons or over the batons when in a crowd, but that didn't always work out for some. I never lost mine thank goodness, but I have been there when it has happened. Those gigantic night sticks can pose a problem to some cops in other ways.

I recall a guy that joined after they dropped the height and weight restrictions, and he was no bullshit, 4 foot 11 inches. I shit you not. His fucking baton almost dragged along the ground. Imagine the picture of him on foot patrols when they paired him up with another guy that was 6 foot 7 inches.

Oh, fuck me, did they get some shit. Luckily, with the introduction of expandable batons, which are a little more discreet and manageable, he would not be chinking metal on the ground, but they would have done nothing to help him in the height department. Not that he needed it, the guy could knuckle, and I guess he had to learn to fight being the shortest cop on the force.

One of my favorite changes was the introduction of pepper spray, which is a lachrymatory agent (a chemical compound that irritates the eyes to cause tears, pain, and temporary blindness) otherwise known as Oleoresin Capsicum or OC spray. Now don't get me wrong, my Glock was my absolute favorite piece of equipment. What's not to like, but it's not like you can use it all that often. You have your scheduled training shoots and pull it out here and there, but the OC spray was used a lot more regularly.

Contrary to popular belief, OC spray is not actually a spray at all. Let's face it, if you are going to "spray" someone, you want to still have some distance between you and them. You can't wait until they get super close, and then let go like you are spraying air freshener. It should really be called OC stream because that's what it is.

You know all your spray bottle cleaning products you have at home, and how they usually have a spray or stream function by turning the nozzle, same with this, only this doesn't have the spray function, just the stream. Anyway . . . spray, stream, I don't fucking care what they call it; it is a very useful tool. It does not work all of the time on everyone, but all in all it is a very effective method of getting control of a person.

Fashion Police

Uniforms have evolved over time, too. If you have read my first book, you might recall how the early policewomen in Australia were attached to the traffic division. They would basically go around to schools carrying a handbag, talking stranger danger. Lucky for me, female police were a bit more functional by the time I joined and I was glad that I could be out among the real action.

When I first started though, we did have to wear culottes (which are the worst fashion disaster of our time) and stockings. Constant ladders in the stockings, cold legs from the knee down and feeling like an absolute dickhead in a fake skirt trying to jump fences, led me to wear long pants. We already had long pants for females, but where I worked in the city nobody wore them.

When I moved out to a country station that was close to the snow fields, none of the girls wore the stupid culottes, and they all wore long pants, even in summer. I started wearing long pants there, and did since that day, and burnt the fucking culottes on a bonfire. I apologize in advance if you are a culotte loving person, but I clearly am not, having suffered them for many years. Rant over.

The uniforms worn then, even for the guys, were more like office attire, but nowadays the uniforms are more militarized and functional. Bullet proof vests are now a staple of the daily uniform, where once upon a time we would just slip them on if we were going to a siege or a shooting. Times have changed, and they are a necessary evil.

They are probably comfortable enough for guys, but back then we didn't have the nice new ones you can get that have moulded areas for a pair of boobs to sit in. Oh no, we had heavy, thick and stiff vests that were hot and bulky, and had Kevlar plates pushing down on your chest. Practical, yes, will stop a knife or a bullet, (not all) but comfortable and functional they were not. Thankfully they have evolved in a major way since then.

I Spy

There is one significant change that I am eternally grateful, I was *not* around to see. And that is the introduction of the body cam. Now I know what you are thinking, they are great because they can exonerate you, they can protect you from accusations, and they can be your friend in evidence, but I would have been in the shit more times than I would like to think, had I had a body cam when I was a cop.

Obviously, if you are wearing one, you have to be more careful of what you say and I suppose you get used to it, but I take my hat off to all those cops out there that have their every word recorded, when their unrecorded word is no longer enough. And don't forget the dash cams recording what happens when you drive. Yep, I would have been in the shit.

Back in the day if a car ran from you, you chased it. Lights, sirens, radio, all going at once. I loved a good vehicle pursuit, but then came the restrictions where only certain vehicles and only certified drivers could actively engage in a pursuit, and the shitbags know this. All because some fuckwits can't drive, and ended up crashing while trying to outrun the cops.

There were a lot of changes in the force in the fifteen years I was there, including the introduction of DNA and collecting samples via buccal swabs, but it wasn't just the equipment and processes that changed. The police themselves and their methods and attitudes changed too. When I joined the force, they were looking for people with common sense, the right attitude and aptitude.

Fast forward and it seems common sense is not that common, and they place more emphasis on a college degree than people with life experience and a few brains. I can honestly say rightly or wrongly, that I witnessed this generate a different type of officer. I get it, they wanted the force to have a certain level of education, to raise the profile of policing as a profession, but it largely attracted book worms with no common sense.

I am not sure if this is a global consensus, but I would be amazed if this issue was solely in my department. I am not trying to demean any-body here, but it changed the face of policing, and cops went from being practical and getting it done, to being theoretical and not knowing how to deal with a challenging incident.

Image Management

Change is necessary to adapt to the shifting demands of policing and most changes are for the better, but in my department, there was one change that really fucked things up for a time. The New South Wales Police Force decided that it wanted to improve its image, around the time that it made a college edu-cation part of the requirements of entry.

They changed the name of the department to the New South Wales Police Service. Come on, a service, really? The department basically went soft, and people knew it, and cops lost a lot of respect. It's not a fucking service, and should never have been called a service, as much as they serve the public. It was just wrong.

That was a bad decision and thankfully, they came to their senses and changed it back to police *force*. That was not the only reason that people started losing respect for police; the times have changed and people just don't have that same level of reverence for police. It's not the only reason respect was lost, but it didn't fucking help things.

Policing is different from now to then, and it went from patrolling the streets and reacting to calls, to being heavily tasked and accounted for, without the flexibility and autonomy they once had. This is largely due to changes in policing models, where proactive intelligence-led policing rather than a reactive model was adopted, due to the changing needs of the community.

The good old days that I had are over and long gone. But when each officer comes through the academy, they will likely think that their days were the good old days, as you can only judge what you know and experience. The stuff I have written about is in my experience only, over fifteen years of being a frontline cop, and I don't speak for anyone else, but I am sure there are plenty out there that put on the uniform that can relate.

Seeing so many changes and new ideas come and go, it does make a person pretty resilient. If you got all bent out of shape about things moving and shifting, sometimes at very short notice, then you would end up a nervous wreck. If you are the type of person that likes the grass to grow under your feet, then policing is not the right place for you.

That being said, resilience is key to making it long term as a cop. And apart from being resilient to change, you have to be resilient to the humans that you serve. That means you become a master at dealing with conflict and confrontation.

So, how do cops deal with conflict, aggressive people and bullshit on the daily? Luckily for me, I love confrontation and my top five tips for dealing with it, and making sure you are heard, are coming right up next chapter!

SHERIFF ORIGIN

The word shire-reeve eventually became the modern English word sheriff. The sheriff (in early England, and metaphorically, in present-day America) is the keeper, or chief, of the county.

CHAPTER TEN

The 'C' Word - Confrontation

Can you imagine someone being a cop who couldn't deal with confrontation? What a shit storm that would be. Cops are basically glorified problem solvers, and I have the right to say that because I was one. I distinctly remember the day when I realized I was sick of being a problem solver and said to the complainant, "What the fuck do you want me to do about it?"

Fuck his stupid complaint about some bullshit, neighbor dispute over his lawnmower, that I could care less about. Unfortunately, time on the job and constantly dealing with people and problems can easily push a cop to say "fuck it," and recognize it's time to go. And that's exactly what I did.

But I do love a good argument, and luckily in my current job as a child abuse investigator, I still get plenty of that action. When assholes want to argue with me, I say bring it on, because their protesting and disputing, is just a plea for more information, and I am happy to give it to them.

We all know what confrontation is, and that it can happen between friends, family members, customers, clients and work colleagues. Pretty much anywhere, at any time. But what is the purpose of confrontation and why do so many people fear it? Personally, I love it, but that's just me and my conditioning to it.

Conflict and Confrontation

Confrontation can strike fear into many, and when it happens, stress and emotions can run very high. When this happens though, usually somebody goes away feeling like they haven't been heard, or things can just turn to complete shit and nobody wins. Remember, the goal of confrontation is to restore the balance, not destroy it.

Conflict is not necessarily a bad thing, and when confrontation is done right, it can bring about change and growth. Being that we can experience conflict and have to confront people at work, at home, in stores, or out in public, it's a good idea to get a handle on how you deal with confrontation yourself.

This way you can enter into a battle feeling empowered, knowing what you want to say, to calmly get your point across and get some resolution. Many people simply avoid confrontation, and would rather be anywhere else, but avoiding it only puts a tighter grip onto the issue you are trying to get rid of.

But what do you do when the thought of approaching someone, or being approached yourself makes you want to piss your pants and run home to momma? You can't avoid confrontation for the rest of your life, unless you are living on a deserted island like Tom Hanks in Castaway. Actually, that's a bad example, because he did have a fight with Wilson, the basketball.

You get the point though, that it's unavoidable. So, if you are a person that does not like confrontation, you have to ask, what is it exactly that makes you so fearful to speak out and stand up for yourself? What will happen if you say something? And what do you fear about confronting someone or someone confronting you?

Are you worried about being yelled at? It's not as though your boss is going to jump across the desk and choke you out for speaking up. (I am certain that has happened somewhere but let's say not, for the purpose of our exercise.) Seriously, what is the worst thing that could happen if you say something?

Furthermore, what are you losing if you keep your mouth shut? Only you can answer that. Well, guess what. When a person goes off and yells and screams at you, they are completely giving up their power to you, because you have obviously pushed their fucking buttons and got a very strong reaction.

I love it, I just sit back and laugh when people start screaming, waving their arms around and talking shit. I don't give a fuck; my blood pressure is intact, while they are having a coronary. It's funny to me. I break out the popcorn in my mind, and watch the show, and when they have run out of air and are starting to slow down, I make my move.

There is an exception to this rule though. If I went to a callout that turned ugly, and had someone behaving badly that needed to be subdued, they would be lucky to get any words out, and would be taken down in a heartbeat. But I am not really talking about confrontation as a cop, just confrontation in general.

Not confronting someone about something that is bothering you can be just as stressful as confronting them. I get it; it's not a nice place to be, but there are ways to get through it, and being that you can't avoid it completely for the rest of your life, you might as well try and get better at it.

Personally, if I have an issue with someone, I get right to it. If I am thinking it, you will know about it. And I like to resolve things quickly. If you are having an issue with a person and you bury it, and let it fester, it can erupt down the track like a volcano, instead of a pimple.

Unresolved issues just snowball and get bigger by the day, so getting into it quickly can often be your best bet. Now, this is not always the case, and sometimes it's better to let sleeping dogs lie, but just for a while. I like to tackle shit head on, but timing can be everything.

So, here are some useful tips for those that hate confrontation. Use them all, or just use the ones that resonate with you. Maybe you can identify with your weak point, so just start there. And these tips can be used in any work or personal situation.

I am not a guru, I don't have a degree in conflict resolution, I have just had more conflict than most would have in a lifetime, due to my cop career. These tips are not by any means an exhaustive list, but these are some of the areas where people go wrong. So, dig in, enjoy, and see if you can improve on your skills to confidently tackle confrontation.

1. **Be prepared.** Plan what you want to say; think about it and rehearse it, if you are not confident enough to wing it. Don't go into a confrontation half cocked, balls out ready to bust the place up. You *will* lose. You will lose control, you will lose respect and most of all you will lose the very thing that you wanted to confront the person about, and they will have won. Think before you speak; know the point you are trying to make,

and make it. You know the old chestnut, if you fail to plan, you plan to fail.

Confrontation is no different. If you crack the shits and decide to storm up to someone and have it out with them, you've got to know what you are going to say. I get it. When someone confronts us or we confront them, we need to feel heard and there is nothing wrong with that, so make your words say something. Make them count. Remember your opinion and your words count as much as the next person's, so don't rush and spew a bunch of bullshit that makes you look like an idiot.

2. **Stay calm**. Before a confrontation, make sure you are in the right frame of mind before you approach it. As in rule one, think about what you want to say, and remove the emotion from it. Normally I would say to deal with the conflict as soon as possible after it has occurred, but that is only if you are

calm. You know the saying, "Don't drive angry," well the same applies here. Don't go and confront someone when you are still pissed off about the situation. Again, if in doubt, refer to rule one so you don't turn yourself inside out, and get nowhere. Stay calm. I can't stress this one enough.

If you are not good at confrontation and you attempt it when you are still angry, I can guarantee you'll likely run it off into a ditch. Likewise, if you are being confronted by someone, stay calm, listen to what they have to say, and try not to react. We are all (mostly) adult here, and surely, we can have an adult conversation. Hear the person out, let them have their say and listen. If you do this, and don't jump in at the first comment that makes you want to blow a gasket, you will notice that you have remained calm which in turn will allow you to get your point across calmly. Remember, raising your voice will raise your emotions and your blood pressure. Don't fucking do it.

3. **Keep on point**. Get straight to the point of the problem, don't beat around the bush. But when you do get to the point stay on it. People go wrong with confrontation when they drag up every bit of bullshit that has ever been said. Stay on track, keep to your point and don't allow yourself to be dragged down into someone else's shit. Once you have made your point, don't harp on it, move on and don't personally attack them. Nothing will derail a civil conversation more than a personal jab. When you are wanting to confront your husband's best mate for talking shit about you, then stick to that point.

Don't dredge up the fact that he is bald, has bad breath and couldn't find a fuck in a brothel. You can't control what might come out of their mouth, but you can control what comes out of yours.

And don't take it personally if they start attacking you; they just haven't learned the art of self-control and being a fucking grownup. Oh, and if you really want to get your own way, don't cross your arms, roll your eyes or sigh as this will instantly fuck things up for you. If they do it, be the bigger person and stick to your point.

4. **Check your attitude**. Before you confront someone, check yourself. Do you know exactly what you want to say, and are you calm and coming from a place of resolution or destruction? What are you bringing to the table? Are you coming with a fuck-you attitude, or are you wanting to calmly get your point across and feel heard? The way you approach the situation will have everything to do with how it turns out. If you are coming in hot, with guns blazing you will likely inflame the situation and achieve nothing. Don't give your power

to that person. You need all the help you can get.

If you are already on the back foot when you approach a person to confront them, you will put them off straight away. The confrontation, and final result, depends on your ability to remain calm, and be clear and confident. If you start to raise your voice, they will start to raise theirs. Trust me on this one. It's almost like when you see someone yawn, and then you can't help but yawn. Same thing. If you start yelling, so will they. If you keep calm, you have a better chance of keeping them calm and on task. It works the other way, too. Have you ever been in a conversation and started whispering because the other person was, and then asked yourselves, "Why are we fucking whispering?"

5. **Pick your battles.** Before you go and confront someone you have to ask

yourself if it is even worth the effort. When I was younger, I would fight at the drop of a hat. I would shred anyone that got in my way or said shit about me. Being a cop soon took care of that because if I reacted to every negative word anybody ever said about me, I would be a blubbering mess. These days, basically, I can't be fucked wasting my energy on idiots. Now don't get me wrong, if you throw shit at me about my family, I will still shred you, but what people say and think about me is none of my business, and not worth my time to care.

Ask yourself, what is my motivation for confronting this person? Is it to get my point across and stick up for what I believe in, or am I just doing it for the sake of it? It's not just about picking your battles; you should also pick your time and place. Like I said before, I prefer to nip things in the bud as soon as possible, but sometimes you just can't. I do remember one occasion where I had been tasked to help someone, and then heard them talking shit, that nobody was helping them. I saw fucking red, and felt like ripping their face off, because I cannot stand bullshit. I hate liars. But I was at work, so I had to shut up and simmer down. I was going to speak to them later, and then a miracle happened. I couldn't be fucking bothered. Case in point!

I hope you have enjoyed this book, and are able to take something away from it. If you have an issue that needs confronting, here's some homework. Grab the tip that jumps out to you the most, or the one you feel you need to work on the most and give it a crack. You might surprise yourself. And remember, your opinion is just as important as the next person's, so make sure you have your say.

Be awesome, be better, bring it every day.

Lethal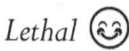

ACKNOWLEDGMENTS

To the New South Wales Police Force, thanks again for the experiences that made this possible.

To my editor, Diann Merit, thanks for getting this book polished up.

To Danijela Mijailovic for the killer cover, and amazing interior design.

To my Launch Team, a massive thanks to those who helped to get this book out there. You helped me more than you know, and it means the world to me to have you involved.

OTHER TITLES
BY THE AUTHOR

GOOD COP

GIRL

C P

The Secret Life of a Police Officer
What you always wanted to know
about policing but were afraid to ask

LISA DOBLE

ABOUT THE AUTHOR

Lisa Doble is an Australian ex-cop, wife, mother and author. She spent fifteen years in the New South Wales Police Force and patrolled the streets in various country and metropolitan locations.

Lisa completed a Bachelor of Social Science, majoring in Counter-Terrorism, Criminology & Forensic Science. She still maintains a strong interest in those topics.

Lisa has published articles in the Australian Police Journal on terrorism topics, including the rise of Foreign Fighters, Radicalization and Violent Extremism.

Lisa has experience in recruitment, where she sought high performing executives for companies within the Guns and Ammunition industry, in the United States.

Lisa had a lifelong dream to write a book and has had that passion since childhood.

When she was about 8 years old, she wrote a book of poems and short stories and decided at that age, that she would one day publish it. She lost the book . . .

Over recent years Lisa has worked in the field of child protection, working in the investigation and assessment team. She has also been conducting family conferencing, both in the government and private sector.

When Lisa is not on the back of a horse, at the gym, or trail running, she is walking the dog, drinking coffee and writing more books.

If you would like to get in touch, Lisa can be found on all forms of social media, or email
contact@lisadoble.com

Firstly, thank you for reading and making it this far. Your support is appreciated.

As a self-published author,
I rely on reviews like yours.

If you loved the book or learned some new stuff, I would be forever grateful if you could leave your honest review on the Amazon page.

This will help more people, like you, to find my book.

Again, thank you so much for the support, until next time....

Lisa Doble 😊

www.lisadoble.com